Level A

Vocabulary

Isabel L. Beck, Ph.D., and
Margaret G. McKeown, Ph.D.

Read-Aloud Anthology

Rigby · Steck-Vaughn

www.HarcourtAchieve.com
1.800.531.5015

Acknowledgments

Editorial Director Stephanie Muller

Lead Editor Terra Tarango

Design Team Cynthia Ellis, Cynthia Hannon, Joan Cunningham

Production Team Mychael Ferris-Pacheco, Paula Schumann, Alan Klemp

Editorial, Design, and Production Development The Quarasan Group, Inc.

Cover Illustration Lori Lohstoeter

Literature

Grateful acknowledgment is given to the following publishers and copyright owners for permissions granted to reprint selections from their publications. All possible care has been taken to trace owner-ship and secure permission for each selection included. In the case of any errors or omissions, the Publisher will be pleased to make suitable acknowledgments in future editions.

p. 1, WORDS ARE LIKE FACES by Edith Baer. Copyright © 1980 by Edith Baer. Reprinted by permission of the author.

p. 7, BIG AL by Andrew Clements, illustrated by Yoshi. Text copyright © 1988 by Andrew Clements. Illustrations copyright © 1988 by Yoshi. Reprinted with permission of Simon & Schuster Books for Young Readers, Simon & Schuster Children's Publishing Division.

p. 13, "One Good Turn Deserves Another" from SILLY & SILLIER: READ-ALOUD RHYMES FROM AROUND THE WORLD by Judy Sierra. Copyright © by Judy Sierra. Used by permission of Alfred A. Knopf, an imprint of Random House Children's Books, a division of Random House, Inc.

p. 19, ALEXANDER AND THE TERRIBLE, HORRIBLE, NO GOOD, VERY BAD DAY by Judith Viorst, illustrated by Ray Cruz. Text copyright © 1997 Judith Viorst. Illustration copyright © 1997 by Ray Cruz. Published by Atheneum Books for Young Readers, Simon & Schuster Children's Publishing Division.

p. 25, "The Frogs Wore Red Suspenders" from THE FROGS WORE RED SUSPENDERS by Jack Prelutsky, illustrated by Petra Mathers. Text copyright © 2002 by Jack Prelutsky. Illustration copyright © 2002 by Petra Mathers. Used by permission of HarperCollins Publishers.

p. 29, "Mr. Bizbee and Miss Doolittle" by Tina Tibbitts from MARVIN COMPOSES A TEA. Copyright © 1988 by Highlights for Children, Inc., Columbus, Ohio.

p. 36, From ONE SMALL GARDEN by Barbara Nichol. Copyright © 2001 by Barbara Nichol. Published by Tundra Books.

p. 44, "The Hen and the Apple Tree" from FABLES by Arnold Lobel. Copyright © 1980 by Arnold Lobel. Used by permission of HarperCollins Publishers.

p. 49, "Spaghetti! Spaghetti!" from RAINY, RAINY SATURDAY by Jack Prelutsky. Text copyright © 1980 by Jack Prelutsky. Used by permission of HarperCollins Publishers.

p. 53, THE LION AND THE LITTLE RED BIRD by Elisa Kleven. Copyright © 1992 by Elisa Kleven. Used by permission of Dutton Children's Books, A division of Penguin Young Readers Group, A Member of Penguin Group (USA) Inc., 345 Hudson St., New York, NY 10014. All rights reserved.

p. 59, "Herbert Glerbett" from THE QUEEN OF EENE by Jack Prelutsky. Text copyright © 1978 by Jack Prelutsky. Used by permission of HarperCollins Publishers.

p. 63, MAMA PROVI AND THE POT OF RICE by Sylvia Rosa-Casanova, illustrated by Robert Roth. Text copyright © 1997 by Sylvia Rosa-Casanova. Illustrations copyright © 1997 by Robert Roth. Reprinted with the permission of Atheneum Books for Young Readers, an imprint of Simon & Schuster Children's Publishing Division.

p. 71, NEVER TRUST A SQUIRREL! by Patrick Cooper, illustrated by Catherine Walters. Text copyright © 1998 by Patrick Cooper. Illustrations copyright © 1998 by Catherine Walters. Used by permission of Dutton Children's Books, A division of Penguin Young Readers Group, A Member of Penguin Group (USA) Inc., 345 Hudson St., New York, NY 10014. All rights reserved.

p. 78, FLIP-FLOPS by Nancy Cote. Text and illustration copyright © 1998 by Nancy Cote. Reprinted by permission of Albert Whitman & Company. All rights reserved.

p. 84, MY BUILDING by Robin Isabel Ahrens, illustrated by Ilja Bereznickas. Text copyright © 1988 by Robin Isabel Ahrens. Illustrations copyright © 1988 by Iljna Bereznickas. Published by Winslow House International, Inc.

p. 89, "Rabbit Counts the Crocodiles" from HOW & WHY STORIES: WORLD TALES KIDS CAN READ AND TELL by Martha Hamilton and Mitch Weiss. Used by permission of Marian Reiner.

p. 101, KISS THE COW! by Phyllis Root, illustrated by Will Hillenbrand. Text copyright © 2000 by Phyllis Root. Illustrations copyright © 2000 by Will Hillenbrand. Reproduced by permission of Candlewick Press, Cambridge, MA.

p. 127, SEAL SURFER by Michael Foreman. Copyright © 1996 by Michael Foreman. Reprinted with permission of Harcourt, Inc.

p. 135, JAMAICA AND THE SUBSTITUTE TEACHER by Juanita Havill, illustrated by Anne Sibley O'Brien. Text copyright © 1999 by Juanita Havill. Illustrations copyright © 1999 by Anne Sibley O'Brien. Reprinted by permission of Houghton Mifflin Company. All rights reserved.

p. 143, AND TO THINK THAT WE THOUGHT THAT WE'D NEVER BE FRIENDS by Mary Ann Hoberman, illustrated by Kevin Hawkes. Text copyright © 1999 by Mary Ann Hoberman. Illustrations copyright © 1999 by Kevin Hawkes. Published by arrangement with Random House Children's Books a division of Random House, Inc., New York, New York, USA. All rights reserved.

Illustrations
Yuri Salzman iii, vi; Teri Weidner v.

Photography
p. vii © Dennis Fagan; p. 37 © Kenneth M. Highfill/Photo Researchers, Inc.; p. 96 © Bettmann/CORBIS.

Contents

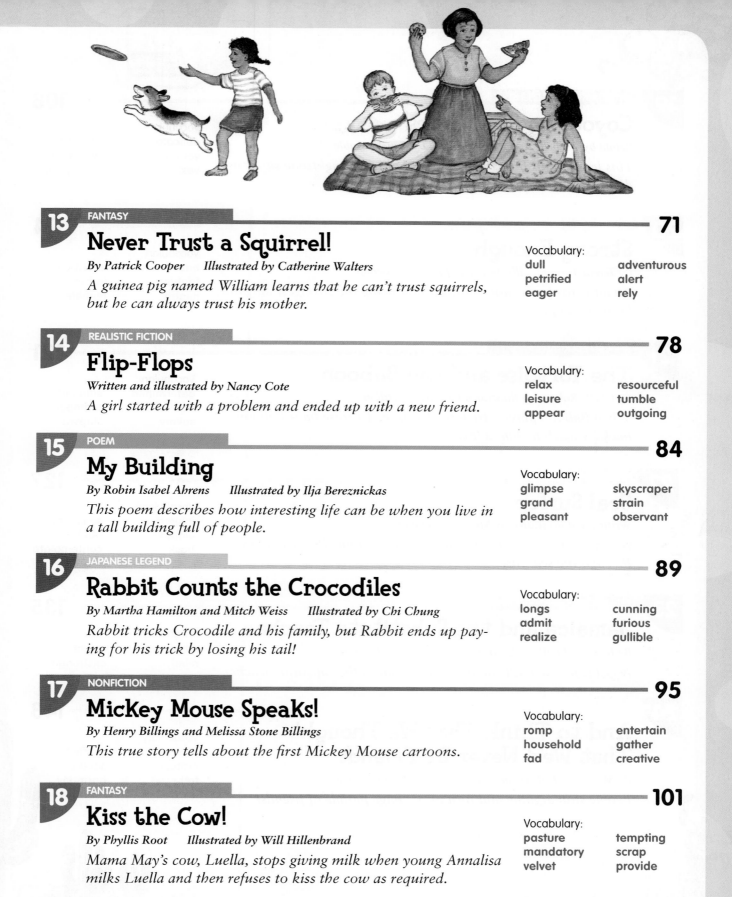

The Magic of Reading Aloud

Research Says. . .

"Read quality literature to students to build a sense of story and to develop vocabulary and comprehension."
—National Reading Panel

Many literate adults have fond memories of being read to as children. This is no coincidence. Reading research has shown that, besides being an enjoyable experience, reading aloud to children is a valuable tool in the teaching of language.

How Reading Aloud Fosters
Vocabulary Development

Children begin understanding a variety of words long before they can read them. A word that could provide a stumbling block to a child reading silently is perfectly comprehensible when the child hears the word spoken and used in context. It follows, then, that a Read-Aloud Anthology is the perfect springboard for vocabulary development.

What This Read-Aloud Does	What This Means for You
Exposes children to rich, sophisticated words used in captivating, age-appropriate stories and poems	You can add a large store of descriptive, robust words and concepts to children's vocabularies.
Provides engaging vocabulary introduction strategies after each read-aloud	You can introduce the vocabulary words in natural and memorable ways as part of your read-aloud discussion.
Encourages children to relate each vocabulary word to their own experiences	You can help children make connections with powerful words—and enjoy hearing them make the words their own!

Bringing the
Story to Life

There you are at center stage! Who, you? A performer? Yes! Just look at your audience, eagerly waiting for you to read them a story. Following some simple tips will help dramatize the performance and make it even more satisfying and valuable for children.

Tips for Reading Aloud

Practice reading ahead of time. Reading stories and poems aloud before reading to children helps you read fluently, with appropriate intonations and expression.

Introduce the story. Before you begin reading, show children the illustration and ask what they think the story will be about.

Build background. If you think there are concepts of the selection that will be unfamiliar, provide enough background to help children understand the reading.

Read expressively. It's difficult to overdramatize when reading to children. Don't be afraid to use plenty of expression to reflect the mood of what you are reading.

Read slowly and clearly. Listeners will be better able to absorb and comprehend what you are saying when they have enough time to form mental images as they listen.

Pace your reading. The best pace is one that fits the story event. If exciting action is taking place, speed up a bit. To build suspense, slow down and lower your voice.

Use props. Bring in or make simple props if they will help clarify or enhance the story.

Involve your listeners. Encourage children to make sound effects or to provide rhyming or repeated words when a pattern has been established.

Ask questions. As you read, ask questions that allow listeners to make connections with their own experiences and to stay engaged.

Listen as you read. Pay attention to children's comments during the story so you can build on those ideas and experiences in discussions after reading.

Enjoy yourself! If you are enthusiastic about what you are reading, children will learn that reading is an enjoyable activity.

Research Says. . .

. . . regular reading aloud strengthens children's reading, writing, and speaking skills—and thus the entire civilizing process.
—The New Read-Aloud Handbook, Jim Trelease

Words Are Like Faces

This poem is a celebration of words, exploring the range of emotions that words express as well as the wonderful sounds they make.

Vocabulary

Words From the Poem

These words appear in blue in the poem. You might wish to go over their meanings briefly before reading the poem.

comforting
Something comforting makes you feel better when you are sad or afraid.

fleet
A person or animal that is fleet moves fast.

glimmer
To glimmer is to shine or twinkle softly.

Words About the Poem

These words will be introduced after the poem is read, using context from the poem.

expression   **lively**   **versatile**

Getting Ready for the Read-Aloud

Show children the picture on page 2 of all the children's faces. Read the title aloud, and point out how each child's face shows how they are feeling. Point out that these children are happy.

Explain that the words people use tell something about how they feel. In this poem the poet talks about how words help people share their feelings.

The following words appear in the poem. You can explain them briefly as you come to them: *penned,* written with a pen; *sheltering,* covering or protecting something to make it safe; *piercing,* sticking something to make a hole in it; *wounding,* hurting.

Words Are Like Faces

By Edith Baer

Illustrated by Lori Lohstoeter

ords can be spoken,
printed or penned,
put on a blackboard
or mailed to a friend,
passed as a secret
from one to another—
words are what people
say to each other.

Words can be plain
like a loaf of fresh bread,
comforting words
like your very own bed,
sheltering words
like the room where you play—
safe, snug and cozy,
and easy to say.

Bringing the Poem to Life

As you read this poem, bring out its rhythm and savor the sounds of each word. Use exaggerated expressions that reflect the emotions described in the poem. You may read the entire poem once, and then read it again, pausing to ask questions.

What kinds of words are "safe, snug and cozy"?

Words can be **fleet** things,
light as a cloud,
lovely to hear
as you say them aloud—
sunlight and rainbow,
snowflake and star—
they **glimmer** and shimmer
and shine from afar.

Words can be arrows
shot from a bow,
piercing and wounding
wherever they go.
Words can be soothing
and healing instead.
Be careful with words,
for they can't be unsaid.

Why does the poet warn us to be careful with words?

Some words are like faces
we've known long before,
and some like new places
to find and explore.
Some twirl on tiptoes,
some clatter or clink,
and some sound exactly
the way you would think!

Do you have favorite
words of your own?
Milkshake or magic?
Old funny bone?
Whippoorwill, daffodil,
merry-go-round?
Touch them and taste them
and try on their sound!

Words tell you're happy,
angry or sad,
make you feel better
when you feel mad,
get off your chest
what you're trying to hide—
Words tell what people
feel deep inside.

Talking About the Poem

- Ask children to tell what they think this poem is about and why the poet wrote it.
- Have children list some of their favorite words and explain what it is they like about them.

Vocabulary in Action

Words From the Poem

comforting

The poem says some words can be comforting, "like your very own bed." Something comforting makes you feel better when you're sad or afraid. Let's say *comforting* together.

- Ask children who needs comforting, someone who just won a new bicycle or someone who fell off their bicycle. Why is that?
- Invite children to discuss things that are comforting to them.

Words About the Poem

expression

The poem describes words as being like faces because faces can show many different feelings. Another way to say that is that words are like expressions. Your expression is the look on your face that shows what you are feeling. Let's say *expression* together.

- Ask where you would look at a person to see their expression, their face or their elbow. Explain.
- Name different feelings (such as happy, sad, angry, and funny) and have children show you what the expression on their face would look like for each feeling.

fleet

The poem says words can be fleet things. This means they can be said quickly. A person or an animal that is fleet moves fast. Let's say *fleet* together.

- Ask which a fleet person would do, catch everyone while playing tag or always get tagged out. Explain your choice.
- Have a child act out how a fleet person would walk to the front of the room.

glimmer

The poem says that words can glimmer. To glimmer is to shine or twinkle softly. Let's say *glimmer* together.

- Ask children which is more likely to glimmer, a star or a tree. Why?
- Give children strips of tinfoil and have them wave the strips back and forth so that they glimmer.

lively

The poem tells us that words are full of life. Another way to say that is to say words are lively. Someone or something that is lively is full of life. Let's say *lively* together.

- Ask which a lively person would do, run nine times around the playground or take a nap under the jungle gym. Tell why.
- Have children act out how a lively person would get out of bed in the morning.

versatile

The poem tells us that words can do many different things. This means that words are versatile. If someone or something is versatile, it can do many different things. Let's say *versatile* together.

- Ask children which is more versatile, a car that can turn into an airplane and fly or a car that can only drive on the road. Explain your answer.
- Ask children to describe a versatile machine that they would like to have, such as a machine that could tie your shoes and cook your breakfast.

Bringing the Story to Life

Emphasize the words *little, big,* and *TEETH* in the third paragraph. When you get to the part where Big Al sneezes, act out a giant sneeze that would be worthy of Big Al!

 n the wide blue sea there was a very friendly fish named Big Al. You could not find a nicer fish. But Big Al also looked very, very, scary.

Other fish seemed to have at least one friend. Some had many. But Big Al had none.

He did not really blame the other fish. How could he expect **little** fish to trust a great **big** fish with eyes and skin and TEETH like his? So Big Al was lonely, and cried big salty tears into the big salty sea.

But Big Al really wanted friends, so he worked at it. First he tried wrapping himself up with seaweed. He thought it was a great disguise, but no one else did. Who wants to stop and talk to a floating plant that has big sharp teeth?

Why doesn't Big Al have any friends?

Then he thought that if he puffed himself up round, the other fish would laugh, and see how clever and silly he could be. All they saw was how BIG he could be, and they steered clear.

Very early one morning, Big Al went down to the bottom and flopped and wiggled himself into the sand until he was almost covered up. He looked much smaller. When other fish came near, Big Al talked and joked with them and had a **delightful** time. But then one scratchy little grain of sand got stuck in his gills—and he...and hehe...and he sn...and he SSSNEEEEEEZED.

When the clouds of sand cleared away, all the other fish were gone.

Big Al even changed his color one day so he could look like he belonged to a school of tiny fish passing by. He bubbled along with them for a while, laughing and feeling like he was just one of the crowd. But he was so big and **clumsy** that when all the tiny fish darted to the left and then quickly back to the right, Big Al just plowed straight ahead. He went bumping and thumping right into the little fish. Before he could even say "Excuse me," they were gone, and he was all alone again, sadder than ever.

Just when Big Al was starting to be sure that he would never have a single friend, something happened. He was floating along sadly watching some of the smaller fish, and was wishing they would come closer. As he watched, a net dropped down silently from above, and in an instant, they were caught.

What just happened to Big Al and the other fish? Where do you think the net came from?

Big Al forgot all about being lonely, and he forgot all about being sad. His eyes bulged out bigger and rounder than ever, and with a mighty flip of his tail he opened his mouth and charged straight at the net! The net was strong, but Big Al was stronger. He ripped right through it, and all the little fish rushed out through the hole.

But when Big Al tried to turn around and go out of the hole, he got all tangled up in the net. He was stuck! The net went higher and higher toward the bright surface of the sea, and the little fish watched Big Al as he disappeared above them. When the little fish were able to speak again, all they talked about was the huge, wonderful fish that had saved them. How great to be free, but what a shame that the big fellow had been **captured**.

> How do the little fish feel about Big Al now?

Just then there was a tremendous, crashing splash above them, and the small fish dashed away. Was it the net again?

Not at all—It was Big Al. Those fishermen took one look at him, and threw him right back into the ocean. And now there is one huge, puffy, scary, **fierce**-looking fish in the sea who has more friends than anyone else: Big Al.

Talking About the Story

- Ask children to describe all the things Big Al did to try to make friends with the other fish. Ask them what Big Al did that finally gave him his wish.
- Ask children if they think everyone needs to be the same size or look the same in order to be friends. Invite children to share what they think makes someone a good friend.

Vocabulary in Action

delightful

When Big Al hides in the sand, he has a delightful time talking and joking with the other fish. If you say someone or something is delightful, you mean it is very pleasant. Let's say *delightful* together.

- Ask children if picking up smelly socks is a delightful thing to do. Why or why not?
- Have children name different activities that they think are delightful.

fierce

Big Al is a fierce-looking fish, but he is really very friendly. A fierce animal or person behaves in a mean way and often looks for a fight. Let's say *fierce* together.

- Ask which animal is fierce, a lion or a lamb? Why do you think so?
- Ask children to think of an animal that is fierce and show how that animal acts.

clumsy

Big Al is clumsy and bumps into the little fish when he tries to swim with them. A clumsy person has trouble moving or handling things and often trips over or breaks them. Let's say *clumsy* together.

- Ask which a clumsy person might do, be a good dancer or step on someone's toes? Explain your answer.
- Ask a child to show how a clumsy person might knock an object off a table.

capture

At the end of the story, Big Al is captured for a little while when he gets tangled in the net. If you capture someone or something, you catch it and keep it from getting away. Let's say *capture* together.

- Ask what is more likely to be captured, a wild animal or a cloud? Explain.
- Have a child pretend to be Big Al and show how he looked when he was captured.

Words About the Story

rescue

Big Al saves the little fish by biting a hole in the net. Another way to say that is to say he rescues the little fish. When you rescue someone, you save them from something bad happening. Let's say *rescue* together.

- Ask whether someone would feel happy or mad after being rescued. Why?
- Ask a child to name some people who often rescue other people, such as lifeguards, firefighters, etc.

suspense

When Big Al gets caught in the net, we are not sure whether or not he will be able to free himself. We are in suspense about whether or not Al will be able to free himself. Suspense is the feeling you get when you know something is about to happen very soon. Let's say *suspense* together.

- Ask children if they are in suspense when they know how a story ends. Why or why not?
- Call on children to act out how they would look if they were watching a very exciting movie and were in suspense about what would happen next.

One Good Turn Deserves Another

In this Mexican folk tale, a mouse saves a snake's life and, with the help of a coyote, proves that one good turn deserves another.

Vocabulary

Words From the Story

These words appear in blue in the story. You might wish to go over their meanings briefly before reading the story.

deserve

If you deserve something, you should get it because of what you have done.

grateful

If you are grateful for something that someone has given you or done for you, you are pleased and wish to thank the person.

amble

When you amble somewhere, you walk there slowly and in a restful way.

plead

If you plead with someone, you beg them to do something for you that will help you out.

Words About the Story

These words will be introduced after the story is read, using context from the story.

deceive   challenge

Getting Ready for the Read-Aloud

Show children the picture on page 14 of the mouse and the snake. Read the title aloud, and tell children that, in this story, a little mouse saves a snake's life. The mouse is then very surprised when the snake wants to eat her!

Tell children that this story is a folk tale, and that folk tales are stories that have been told for many years. Tell them that this folk tale is from the country of Mexico. Use a map or globe to point out where Mexico is in relation to where you live.

You might want to explain the meanings of these words as you come to them in the story: *evil, armadillo,* and *coyote. Evil* is something that is very bad. An *armadillo* is a small animal that is covered with a very tough shell. A *coyote* is an animal that looks very much like a big dog.

One Good Turn Deserves Another

A Mexican folk tale retold by Judy Sierra
Illustrated by Ruth Flanigan

Hop, stop, sniff. Hop, stop, sniff. A mouse was going across the desert. Suddenly, she heard a voice, "Help! Help me!" The sound came from under a rock. "Plea*sssse* get me out of here," said the voice, with an unmistakable hiss.

The mouse placed her front paws against the rock. She was small, but she gave it her best. The rock rolled aside and out slid a snake.

"Thank you *ssso* much," said the snake as he curled a coil around the mouse. "I was stuck under that rock for a long time. I am very hungry."

"But you wouldn't eat *me*," squeaked the mouse.

"Why not?" the snake asked.

"Because I moved the rock," said the mouse. "I saved your life."

"So?" hissed the snake.

"So, one good turn **deserves** another," the mouse said hopefully.

The snake moved his head from side to side. "You are young," he said. "You don't know much about the world. Good is often repaid with evil."

"That's not fair!" cried the mouse.

"Everyone knows I am right," said the snake. "If you find even one creature who agrees with you, I will set you free."

Bringing the Story to Life

As you read the part of the snake, extend the *s* in words like *ssso* to make the snake hiss. Use a high, squeaky voice for the mouse. For the crow, use a bored, matter-of-fact voice. Read the armadillo's words with a slow, lumbering voice. Try to make the coyote's voice sound tricky or mischievous.

> What does the mouse mean by "one good turn deserves another"?

> What does the snake mean by "good is often repaid with evil"?

A crow alighted on a nearby bush.

"Uncle," said the snake to the crow, "help us settle an argument. I was trapped under a rock, and this silly mouse set me free. Now she thinks I shouldn't eat her."

"He should be **grateful**," the mouse insisted.

"Well, now," said the crow. "I've flown high and I've flown low. I've been just about everywhere. This morning, I ate some grasshoppers that were destroying a farmer's crops. Was he grateful? No. He used me for target practice! Good is often repaid with evil." And off he flew.

Why did the crow agree with the snake?

An armadillo **ambled** by. "What's all the noise?" she asked.

"Merely a short conversation before dinner," replied the snake. "My young friend moved a rock and set me free. Now she thinks I shouldn't eat her."

"One good turn deserves another," said the mouse.

"Wait a minute," said the armadillo. "Did you know he was a snake before you moved that rock?"

"I guess I did, but…"

"A snake is always a snake," the armadillo declared as she waddled away.

"That settles it," said the snake. "Everyone agrees with me."

"Can't we ask just one more creature?" the mouse **pleaded**.

"I don't think you'll ever understand," groaned the snake.

A coyote trotted up. "Understand what?" he asked.

"The snake was trapped under that rock," the mouse explained.

"Which rock?" asked the coyote.

"Over there. That rock," said the snake.

"Oh," said the coyote. "The mouse was under that rock."

"No, *I* was under that rock!" said the snake.

"A snake under a rock? Impossible," the coyote snorted. "I have never seen such a thing."

The snake slid into the hole where he had been trapped. "I was in this hole," he hissed, "and that rock was on top of me!"

"This rock?" the coyote asked as she lifted her paw and pushed the rock on top of the snake.

"Ye*sss*!" hissed the snake. "Now show him, little mouse! Show him how you set me free."

But the mouse was already far away. "Thank you, cousin," she called as she ran. "I'll return the favor someday."

"Yes, indeed," said the coyote. "One good turn deserves another."

What did the coyote do to help the mouse?

Talking About the Story

- Ask children to tell what the mouse and coyote each thought about doing good things for others. Ask how that was different from what the snake thought.
- Ask children which animal they agree with. Invite them to talk about times when they have done something good for someone or when someone has done something good for them.

Vocabulary in Action

deserve

In the story the mouse thought she deserved to go free because she saved the snake's life. If you deserve something, you should get it because of what you have done. Let's say *deserve* together.

- Ask children if a child who helps clean the garage deserves to go to a party or to get in trouble. Why?
- Call on volunteers to tell about a time when they got something they deserved.

plead

The mouse pleads with the snake to ask just one more creature what they think. If you plead with someone, you beg them to do something for you that will help you out. Let's say *plead* together.

- Ask if children would be more likely to plead for a new toy or to go throw out the trash. Why?
- Ask children to show how they would act if they were pleading with a parent to let them stay up a little later.

grateful

The mouse thought that the snake should be grateful that she saved his life. If you are grateful for something that someone has given you or done for you, you are pleased and wish to thank the person. Let's say *grateful* together.

- Ask children if a grateful person would say "thank you" or "I'm sorry." Explain.
- Have children think of someone they are grateful for and have them write a brief note to the person.

amble

In the story an armadillo ambles by while the mouse and snake are talking. When you amble somewhere, you walk there slowly and in a restful way. Let's say *amble* together.

- Ask whether you would amble if you were late to school or if you were early. Explain your answer.
- Call on volunteers to amble around the classroom.

deceive

At the end of the story, the coyote makes the snake think he doesn't understand what happened in order to get him back under the rock. The coyote deceived the snake. If you deceive someone, you make them believe something that is not true. Let's say *deceive* together.

- Ask children if they deceive someone, do they fool the person or tell the truth. Explain.
- Ask children to tell about a time they deceived someone or they were deceived.

challenge

The snake told the mouse that if she could find one creature who agreed with her, he would set her free. Another way to say that is to say the snake challenged the mouse to find a creature who agreed with her. If you challenge someone, you ask them to do something that is difficult or that you think they cannot do. Let's say *challenge* together.

- Ask what would challenge you more, eating breakfast with a large family or cooking a huge breakfast for all of them. Why?
- Have children share stories about times when they were challenged by something.

Alexander and the Terrible, Horrible, No Good Very Bad Day

In this story a boy tells about a very bad day when everything goes wrong.

Vocabulary

Words From the Story

These words appear in blue in the story. You might wish to go over their meanings briefly before reading the story.

scrunched
If something is scrunched, it gets pushed together and squeezed.

invisible
If something is invisible, you can't see it.

scold
If you scold someone, you say angry things to them about something they have done.

Words About the Story

These words will be introduced after the story is read, using context from the story.

dreadful   **complain**   **exaggerate**

Getting Ready for the Read-Aloud

Show children the picture of Alexander getting out of bed on page 20. Read the title aloud, and tell children that *terrible, horrible,* and *no good* are all different ways to say that Alexander is having a very bad day. Ask what they see in the picture that shows that his day has started badly.

Explain that when people have a bad day, they often feel like running away. When bad things keep happening to Alexander, he wants to run away to Australia. You may want to use a map or globe to show children just how far away Australia is from where they are.

As you encounter these words in the story, explain them briefly: *cavity,* a small hole in a tooth that a dentist needs to fill; *copying machine,* a machine that makes copies of pages.

Alexander and the Terrible, Horrible, No Good Very Bad Day

By Judith Viorst

Illustrated by Ray Cruz

I went to sleep with gum in my mouth and now there's gum in my hair and when I got out of bed this morning I tripped on the skateboard and by mistake I dropped my sweater in the sink while the water was running and I could tell it was going to be a terrible, horrible, no good, very bad day.

At breakfast Anthony found a Corvette Sting Ray car kit in his breakfast cereal box and Nick found a Junior Undercover Agent code ring in his breakfast cereal box but in my breakfast cereal box all I found was breakfast cereal.

I think I'll move to Australia.

In the car pool Mrs. Gibson let Becky have a seat by the window. Audrey and Elliot got seats by the window too. I said I was being **scrunched**. I said I was being smushed. I said, if I don't get a seat by the window I am going to be carsick. No one even answered.

I could tell it was going to be a terrible, horrible, no good, very bad day.

—————— ★ ★ ★ ——————

At school Mrs. Dickens liked Paul's picture of the sailboat better than my picture of the **invisible** castle.

At singing time she said I sang too loud. At counting time she said I left out sixteen. Who needs sixteen?

I could tell it was going to be a terrible, horrible, no good, very bad day.

Bringing the Story to Life

Use your voice to animate Alexander's mounting frustration with each terrible event. Every time you say the phrase "terrible, horrible, no good, very bad day," inject a whining tone to your voice for a humorous effect.

What made Alexander think he was going to have a terrible day before he even got to school?

I could tell because Paul said I wasn't his best friend anymore. He said that Philip Parker was his best friend and that Albert Moyo was his next best friend and that I was only his third best friend.

I hope you sit on a tack, I said to Paul. I hope the next time you get a double-decker strawberry ice-cream cone the ice cream part falls off and lands in Australia.

There were two cupcakes in Philip Parker's lunch bag and Albert got a Hershey bar with almonds and Paul's mother gave him a piece of jelly roll that had little coconut sprinkles on the top. Guess whose mother forgot to put in dessert?

It was a terrible, horrible, no good, very bad day.

That's what it was, because after school my mom took us all to the dentist and Dr. Fields found a cavity just in me. Come back next week and I'll fix it, said Dr. Fields.

Next week, I said, I'm going to Australia.

On the way downstairs the elevator door closed on my foot and while we were waiting for my mom to go get the car Anthony made me fall where it was muddy and then when I started crying because of the mud Nick said I was a crybaby and while I was punching Nick for saying crybaby my mom came back with the car and **scolded** me for being muddy and fighting.

I am having a terrible, horrible, no good, very bad day, I told everybody. No one even answered.

> Do you think the things that happened to Alexander were terrible? Why or why not?

So then we went to the shoestore to buy some sneakers. Anthony chose white ones with blue stripes. Nick chose red ones with white stripes. I chose blue ones with red stripes but then the shoe man said, We're all sold out. They made me buy plain old white ones, but they can't make me wear them.

When we picked up my dad at his office he said I couldn't play with his copying machine, but I forgot. He also said to watch out for the books on his desk, and I was careful as I could be except for my elbow. He also said don't fool around with his phone, but I think I called Australia. My dad said please don't pick him up anymore.

It was a terrible, horrible, no good, very bad day.

What happened to Alexander at his dad's office?

There were lima beans for dinner and I hate limas.

There was kissing on TV and I hate kissing.

My bath was too hot, I got soap in my eyes, my marble went down the drain, and I had to wear my railroad-train pajamas. I hate my railroad-train pajamas.

When I went to bed Nick took back the pillow he said I could keep and the Mickey Mouse night-light burned out and I bit my tongue.

The cat wants to sleep with Anthony, not with me.

It has been a terrible, horrible, no good, very bad day.

Mom says some days are like that.

Even in Australia.

Talking About the Story

- Ask children to recall as many terrible things as they can that happened to Alexander. Encourage them to tell the events in the order in which they happened.
- Ask children whether they have ever had a terrible day like Alexander's. Invite them to tell what their day was like.

Vocabulary in Action

Words From the Story

scrunched

In the story Alexander got scrunched in the car. If something is scrunched, it gets pushed together and squeezed. Let's say *scrunched* together.

- Ask a child to explain how dirty clothes might get scrunched in a laundry basket.
- Have four children act out what it would be like to be scrunched on a small bench.

invisible

Alexander drew an invisible castle. If something is invisible, you can't see it. Let's say *invisible* together.

- Ask which is invisible, air or an airplane. Why?
- Call on a child to draw a picture of someone walking an invisible dog.

scold

Alexander's mom scolded him for fighting with his brother. If you scold someone, you say angry things to them about something they have done. Let's say *scold* together.

- Ask which might you get scolded for, doing your homework or forgetting to clean your room. Explain.
- Have a child act out scolding a pet.

Words About the Story

dreadful

Alexander was having a terrible, horrible day. You could say he was having a dreadful day. If something is dreadful, it is so terrible that it could not be much worse. Let's say *dreadful* together.

- Ask which might make your day dreadful, losing a new sweater in the park or wearing a new sweater to the park. Why?
- Ask children to show the face they would make if they tasted something dreadful.

complain

Alexander talked a lot about all the bad things that happened. Another way to say that is to say he complained. Complain means to talk about how the things that are happening are bad or unfair. Let's say *complain* together.

- Ask which would make you complain, going to bed early or going to bed late. Explain.
- Call on children to complain about the kind of weather they don't like.

exaggerate

Alexander made things sound much worse than they were. This means he exaggerated. Exaggerate means to make things seem much better or much worse than they really are. Let's say *exaggerate* together.

- Ask which one is exaggerating, saying you see lots of birds or millions of birds. Why?
- Have children act out exaggerating being happy and then sad.

The Frogs Wore Red Suspenders

In this silly poem, a group of animals puts on an unusual performance.

Vocabulary

Words From the Poem

These words appear in blue in the poem. You might wish to go over their meanings briefly before reading the poem.

suspend
When you suspend something, you hold it up or hang it up off the ground.

serenade
If you serenade someone, you sing or play a song for them on a musical instrument.

spangled
Something that is spangled is covered with small, shiny things.

pride
Pride is the feeling you get when you have done something well.

Words About the Poem

These words will be introduced after the poem is read, using context from the poem.

ridiculous   **perform**

Getting Ready for the Read-Aloud

Display pages 26 and 27 and ask what is strange about this picture. Read the title aloud, and ask whether children think this poem will tell about real animals or about make-believe animals and why.

Explain that sometimes poetry can be serious, and that other times it can be silly and fun. Tell children that this poem is not at all serious and tells about a very unusual group of animals. In this poem all the animals do things you would not expect them to do.

Have children prepare for this poem by demonstrating the sounds of frogs, pigs, chickens, and ducks.

The Frogs Wore Red Suspenders

By Jack Prelutsky

Illustrated by Petra Mathers

The frogs wore red **suspenders**
and the pigs wore purple vests,
as they sang to all the chickens
and the ducks upon their nests.

They croaked and oinked a **serenade**,
the ducks and chickens sighed,
then laid enormous **spangled** eggs,
and quacked and clucked with **pride**.

Bringing the Poem to Life

Have fun reading this poem. Use your voice to express surprise at the animal costumes, to dramatize the croaking and oinking, and to demonstrate the sighs of the ducks and chickens. On the last line, act out the birds' pride.

Talking About the Poem

- Ask children to describe the silly things that each animal in this poem did.
- Ask children what they did and did not like about this poem. Ask whether they prefer to listen to poems or stories and why.

27

Vocabulary in Action

suspend

In the poem the frogs wore suspenders. Suspenders are used to hold up pants. When you suspend something, you hold it up or hang it up off the ground. Let's say *suspend* together.

- Ask which you would suspend, a picture on a wall or a carpet on the floor. Why is that?
- Ask children to suspend a pencil or a crayon in the air.

spangled

The ducks and chickens were proud of their spangled eggs. Something that is spangled is covered with small, shiny things. Let's say *spangled* together.

- Ask whether a spangled egg would be bright and sparkly or plain and dull. Why?
- Have children work in groups to create spangled eggs. Give each group a white piece of paper, a glue stick, and some sequins and glitter. Display their spangled eggs around the classroom.

serenade

The frogs and pigs serenaded the ducks and chickens. If you serenade someone, you sing or play a song for them on a musical instrument. Let's say *serenade* together.

- Ask children which person might be serenading, someone playing the piano or someone playing soccer. Explain your answer.
- Have half the class serenade the other half by singing a song they all know.

pride

At the end of the poem, the ducks and chickens clucked with pride. Pride is the feeling you get when you have done something well. Let's say *pride* together.

- Ask children which would give them pride, being sick or having a teacher tell you that you did a great job. Explain.
- Ask children to tell about something they have done that gave them pride.

Words About the Poem

ridiculous

The poem told about animals that did very strange and silly things. You could also say they did ridiculous things. Something ridiculous is very foolish and makes no sense. Let's say *ridiculous* together.

- Ask which would be ridiculous, a kite with a string or a kite that could talk. Why?
- Ask children to make a ridiculous face at you.

perform

The pigs and frogs sang for the ducks and chickens. Another way to say that is to say the pigs and frogs performed. When you perform, you do something like sing, dance, play an instrument, or speak in front of a group. Let's say *perform* together.

- Ask where someone might perform, in a closet or on a stage. Explain.
- Ask several children at a time to stand and perform a silly dance for the group.

Mr. Bizbee and Miss Doolittle

In this story two neighbors who are very different find they have some things in common after all.

Vocabulary

Words From the Story

These words appear in blue in the story. You might wish to go over their meanings briefly before reading the story.

tidy
Something that is tidy is very neat and clean.

irk
If you irk someone, you make them a little bit angry.

admire
When you admire someone, you look up to them and want to be like them. When you admire something, you like looking at it.

chuckle
When you chuckle, you laugh quietly.

Words About the Story

These words will be introduced after the story is read, using context from the story.

astonished   coincidence

Getting Ready for the Read-Aloud

Show children the picture on pages 30 and 31 of *Mr. Bizbee and Miss Doolittle*. Read the title aloud, and tell children that in this story, two neighbors who are very different have trouble getting along.

Explain that French is a language that is spoken in countries such as France and Canada and parts of Africa, such as Senegal. You may want to point out these countries on a map or globe.

Tell children that the phrase "a bumper crop of weeds" means "a lot of weeds." Also explain that a tuba is a large musical instrument that has a very deep tone.

Mr. Bizbee and Miss Doolittle

By Tina Tibbitts
Illustrated by Meg Aubrey

Mr. Bizbee lived in the **tidiest** house in town. The grass around it was always trimmed. Even the flowers stood up straight in their beds. Mr. Bizbee would not have had it any other way.

One day someone moved into the empty house next door. Mr. Bizbee decided to go over and say hello.

"I'm Miss Doolittle," said the new neighbor. "And this is my cat, Snoozy."

"May I help you unpack your boxes?" asked Mr. Bizbee.

"No, thanks," Miss Doolittle replied. "Whenever I need something, I'll unpack it."

"Perhaps I could mow your lawn," offered Mr. Bizbee.

"Mowing the lawn is a waste of time," replied Miss Doolittle. "Besides, long grass and wildflowers are pretty."

Read Mr. Bizbee's dialogue in a formal tone of voice to reflect his personality. Read Miss Doolittle's dialogue in a more casual and friendly tone. As you read the narration, use your voice to reflect the mounting tension between the neighbors.

How are Mr. Bizbee and Miss Doolittle different so far?

After that, Mr. Bizbee did not go over to talk to Miss Doolittle. They clearly did not think alike. Soon they began to **irk** one another.

Blooming in Miss Doolittle's yard were what Mr. Bizbee called weeds. The wind blew their seeds into Mr. Bizbee's yard. Then he had a bumper crop of weeds. He sweated for hours, pulling them up while Miss Doolittle sat in her yard **admiring** the butterflies.

One day Mr. Bizbee put freshly baked bread out on the porch to cool. Miss Doolittle's cat, Snoozy, jumped up on the table and curled up between the warm loaves of bread. When Mr. Bizbee saw this, he grabbed Snoozy and took him over to Miss Doolittle. He told her that cat hairs were all over his wonderful bread. She replied that he never should have left the bread out where Snoozy could get near it.

A month later, as Miss Doolittle unpacked a box to get out the mop, she found her old tuba. She began tooting it every day with the windows of her house open. Mr. Bizbee wore earmuffs to shut out the noise.

Then Mr. Bizbee began learning French. Every evening he sat on his back porch listening to his French records. The records said the same words over and over. Miss Doolittle got tired of hearing the records and went out to tell him so. Mr. Bizbee said something. Miss Doolittle didn't understand French, but it sounded rude to her. She stomped into her house, slamming the door.

> What did Miss Doolittle do that bothered Mr. Bizbee? What did Mr. Bizbee do that bothered Miss Doolittle?

Things did not change until one afternoon in autumn. Mr. Bizbee was putting candles on his birthday cake. He felt silly having it by himself, but he had forgotten to invite anyone over. And it was too late now.

Suddenly he heard Miss Doolittle playing "Happy Birthday" on her tuba. Mr. Bizbee could hardly believe his ears. How could she know about his birthday? Although she had strange ideas, Miss Doolittle might yet perhaps be a kind person. Mr. Bizbee decided to go over and share his cake with her.

> What did Mr. Bizbee think when he heard Miss Doolittle playing "Happy Birthday" on her tuba?

When Miss Doolittle opened her door, she nearly dropped her tuba. There stood Mr. Bizbee holding a birthday cake with candles blazing. Too surprised to speak, she waved him inside.

"First, Miss Doolittle, let me thank you for cheering me up by playing 'Happy Birthday' on your tuba," said Mr. Bizbee.

"I didn't think you liked my tuba playing," replied Miss Doolittle. "And thank you for making me a birthday cake! How did you ever know?"

Mr. Bizbee stared at her. "I made the cake for my birthday," he said.

"And I played 'Happy Birthday' to myself on the tuba," said Miss Doolittle.

Then they both had a good laugh.

Why did Mr. Bizbee and Miss Doolittle laugh?

"Do you like chocolate cake?" asked Mr. Bizbee, still **chuckling**.

"It's my favorite kind," replied Miss Doolittle.

So together they had a double birthday party. Even Snoozy joined the fun.

And since that special birthday, Mr. Bizbee and Miss Doolittle have never let their different ways of thinking keep them from being friends.

Talking About the Story

- Ask children to describe the things that were different about Mr. Bizbee and Miss Doolittle. Ask what the neighbors discovered they shared at the end of the story.

- Ask children if they think people need to think alike or do everything in the same way in order to be friends. Have them explain their answers and share personal experiences.

Vocabulary in Action

tidy

In the story Mr. Bizbee lived in a very tidy house. In fact, it was the tidiest house in town. Something that is tidy is very neat and clean. Let's say *tidy* together.

- Ask children whether a garbage truck is tidy. Why or why not?
- Have children act like Mr. Bizbee and make their desk as tidy as possible.

admire

Miss Doolittle sat in her yard and admired the butterflies. When you admire someone, you look up to them and want to be like them. When you admire something, you like looking at it. Let's say *admire* together.

- Ask children if they would throw away something that they admired. Why or why not?
- Have a child pretend to be Miss Doolittle and show how she looked as she sat in her yard admiring the butterflies.

irk

Mr. Bizbee and Miss Doolittle irk one another. If you irk someone, you make them a little bit angry. Let's say *irk* together.

- Ask children what would irk them, someone holding the door open for them or someone blocking the door so others cannot get by. Why?
- Ask children to show how they would look if they were irked.

chuckle

Mr. Bizbee chuckles about the birthday mix-up. When you chuckle, you laugh quietly. Let's say *chuckle* together.

- Ask children if they would chuckle when they heard a joke or when they lost their favorite shirt. Why?
- Reread the section on page 34 about the birthday mix-up. Chuckle as you read and point out any students who are chuckling.

astonished

Mr. Bizbee was very surprised when he heard Miss Doolittle playing "Happy Birthday" on her tuba. Another way to say that is to say he was astonished. If you are astonished, something has surprised you so much that you feel shocked. Let's say *astonished* together.

- Ask if they would be astonished if an elephant walked into the classroom. Why or why not?
- Ask children to make a face to show they are astonished.

coincidence

When Mr. Bizbee hears Miss Doolittle playing "Happy Birthday" on her tuba, he brings his birthday cake to her house. That's when they find out they have the same birthday! This is an example of a coincidence. A coincidence is when two things just happen but seem like they go together. Let's say *coincidence* together.

- Ask if it is a coincidence if you and your best friend both went to school or if you and your best friend both wore the same exact outfit to school. Explain.
- Call on two children to role-play Mr. Bizbee and Miss Doolittle when they discover the coincidence about their birthdays.

One Small Garden

This excerpt from a nonfiction story solves a mystery about a family of raccoons that comes and goes in a garden.

Vocabulary

Words From the Story

These words appear in blue in the story. You might wish to go over their meanings briefly before reading the story.

survive
To survive is to continue to live, even through difficult times and events.

shelter
To shelter something is to keep it from getting hurt by the sun or the weather.

disturb
When you disturb someone or something, you bother or upset it in some way.

destroy
To destroy something is to break or hurt it so badly that it can't be fixed.

Words About the Story

These words will be introduced after the story is read, using context from the story.

observe   **dwell**

Getting Ready for the Read-Aloud

Show children the photo on page 37 of two raccoons climbing up a tree. Read the title aloud, and explain that this story tells about a raccoon family that wanders through a garden every night and then disappears.

Explain that this is a nonfiction, informational story. It tells about true things that happened. It is also a mystery story because the person telling the story discovers why something strange is happening.

These words appear in the story. You may need to briefly explain them as you come to them: *dawdle*, to do something slowly; *grope*, to feel with your hands, looking for something you can't see; *silhouette*, a dark outline seen against a light background; *endeavors*, hard work.

One Small Garden

By Barbara Nichol

The Raccoon Family

Ten years ago, in the early morning, there would often be raccoons roaming the garden. This was at dawn, when most people are still asleep.

Raccoons go about their business at night. They leave their homes after dark and go out to accomplish the things they need to, to carry on their lives: to eat and to **survive**. Because, for the most part, we do these things by day, we don't often see raccoons. It's easy to forget they're all around us, living with us in the city, so nearby.

In the very early morning, though, the raccoons would sometimes dawdle in the gardens on their way home to sleep. They would stop on the roof of a garage next to the garden—a flat roof covered by a vine.

The vine still grows there and now covers the whole roof…. The littlest raccoons would take their time in the [vine], picking through the leaves and berries. The grown raccoons would wait for the little ones to come along. When the young raccoons had caught up, the raccoon family would climb down the side of a tall tree at the corner of the garage, the big raccoons going first. The little raccoons would grope about the trunk before beginning the climb down to the fence that led them home. They were nervous about climbing straight down. The grown raccoons would wait. It was a short climb down the tree—only about three feet—but straight down.

Bringing the Story to Life

Pause frequently to be sure children understand what is happening. As you read, sketch the garage roof, the tree, and the fence on the board. Use a raccoon cutout to show how the raccoons moved.

Why don't people often see raccoons?

Then, in a slow line, the family would travel along the fence top: big and small, identical shapes in different sizes, round and peaceful, not knowing they were being watched, five or six raccoons in silhouette.

And then they would just seem to disappear. One moment they would be there on the fence and then they would be gone completely, disappearing in the leaves. It was impossible to catch the moment when they left the garden. They seemed to vanish into the pink air.

The Line of Ants

There was a maple tree just inside the gate. The tree was very tall—as tall as a three- or four-story house. Its limbs reached up high and spread out over the garden. In the summer it **sheltered** the garden under green leaves…. One visitor to the garden called the maple tree the guardian of the garden. It seemed to protect the garden under its boughs.

If the tree hadn't been right beside the gate where people come and go, no one would have noticed the line of ants going about their business on the bark—hundreds of them, making their way around the base of the tree and up the trunk. They would disappear into the bark. They would disappear like the raccoons.

> Where could the ants be going?

They always seemed to be there, orderly and busy, hard at work.

The store that sells young plants and tools for gardens is called a nursery. At the nursery they explained that the ants had made a home inside the tree. They said that this could harm the tree….

The Tree Expert[1]

The ants continued their endeavors on the maple, circling and climbing on the trunk.

[An] expert came to see the tree. He stood beneath it, quiet, for some time. He watched their busy progress up and down the trunk. He looked at the vast limbs above the garden, the wealth of tossing rustling leaves.

"The tree looks fine at first," he said, but then he pointed up to something no one else had seen. Partway up the tree were scraps of crumbled old cement, clinging to a hollow in the trunk. Someone, long ago, had tried to patch the tree trunk with cement.

"The tree looks fine at first," he said, "but don't be fooled by tossing rustling leaves. It's possible," he said, "the layers just inside the bark—the layers taking food and water up and down the trunk—are healthy. And so the leaves are green. It could be, though, the tree is weak inside. It's possible the tree looks fine," he said, "and still has hollow places in the trunk. The ants are living there and we don't know how big a home they've found. The tree could be too weak to stand up to a wind or heavy snow. Large pieces could break off, or it could fall."

> Why does the tree expert think the tree might fall?

He said that in the country, it sometimes is all right to leave a tree to fall down on its own. "A city tree should be cut down," he said. "A city tree could fall into a house. Someone could be hurt."

"This tree is very old," he said. "With winter coming on, I would suggest the tree be taken down."

---

[1] This selection is titled "The Second Tree Expert" in the complete work, One Small Garden by Barbara Nichol.

The Day the Tree Came Down

The day the maple tree came down, two men arrived that morning. One of them climbed up high into the tree. He hoisted up a chain saw—a saw with a loud motor— and some ropes. He took off limbs and branches with the saw and, with the ropes, he lowered all the pieces to the ground.

The other man, below, cut the limbs to pieces. He stacked them up like firewood along the path. By lunchtime most of the tree was on the ground. The limbs were gone and just the trunk remained. It was a tall trunk left standing, much taller than the tallest man, but it was here the men were forced to finish for the day. It seems there was a problem. The trunk, you see, was hollow— more frail by far than anyone had guessed. It would indeed have fallen before long. But there was something else as well.

> What do you think might be inside the hollow tree?

Looking up from down inside the trunk were faces, a host of gleaming eyes, set behind long snouts. It was the raccoon family. This hollow tree had been their home. The hollow part was large enough for all of them to live inside.

The men explained they had two choices. They could **disturb** the family—take a pole and push it in the hollow trunk and tease the family so they'd run away. Or they could put their tools away for now and go away themselves. The raccoons, they said, would move out on their own now that their home was open to the sky. Their shelter was **destroyed**.

And so the men packed up and left. They stayed away a week or two. When they came back, the raccoons had moved on.

The men cut down the trunk the day that they returned. And then another worker came and ground the stump out of the earth. She used a loud machine that gave off smoke and smelled of gas.

And this is how we found out why the raccoon family, who disappeared each dawn, had always seemed to vanish into air. We found out why we'd never seen them leave. The reason we now know: they never left. They'd climbed into the branches of the tree and dropped into an opening that none of us had even known was there….

Where have the raccoons gone? We'll never know. They've moved their story off to somewhere else.

Talking About the Story

- Ask children to explain why the tree in the garden was important to the raccoon family.
- Ask children what animals they have seen or read about that live outside.

Vocabulary in Action

Words From the Story

survive

The story tells about raccoons doing things they need to do to survive. To survive is to continue to live, even through difficult times and events. Let's say *survive* together.

- Ask which would survive, a fish in a pond or a fish in a hot oven. Why is that?
- Have children discuss things they need to survive, such as food, sleep, and a place to live.

disturb

The tree cutters did not want to disturb the raccoon family. When you disturb someone or something, you bother or upset it in some way. Let's say *disturb* together.

- Ask which might disturb someone, bringing them a glass of water or tripping and spilling water on them. Why?
- Ask children to describe noises in the night that might disturb them when they are trying to sleep.

shelter

The big tree sheltered the garden. To shelter something is to keep it from getting hurt by the sun or the weather. Let's say *shelter* together.

- Ask children which would shelter you from the sun, a big hat or a happy face sticker. Explain.
- Have two children stand and one child sit between them. Ask the standing children to bend over to shelter the third.

destroy

The raccoons moved when their shelter was destroyed. To destroy something is to break or hurt it so badly that it can't be fixed. Let's say *destroy* together.

- Ask what you should do with something that has been destroyed, give it to some-one as a gift or throw it away. Explain your answer.
- Give a child a piece of paper and have them demonstrate how to destroy it.

Words About the Story

observe

In this story the narrator watches the raccoons. Another way to say that is that the narrator observes the raccoons. To observe something is to watch it very closely. Let's say *observe* together.

- Ask children which you would do if you were observing something, study it or not pay attention to it. Why?
- Ask children to tell about some things they like to observe.

dwell

The raccoons were living inside the tree trunk. Another way to say that is that they were dwelling there. If you dwell somewhere, you live there. Let's say *dwell* together.

- Ask where people might dwell, in the sky or on a hill. Explain your choice.
- Invite children to discuss the place where they dwell.

The Hen and the Apple Tree

In this fable a wolf tries unsuccessfully to trick a clever hen into believing he is an apple tree.

Vocabulary

Words From the Story

These words appear in blue in the story. You might wish to go over their meanings briefly before reading the story.

certain
If you are certain about something, you strongly believe that it is true.

quiver
To quiver means to shake a tiny bit.

outsmart
When you outsmart someone, you trick them or beat them by doing something clever.

Words About the Story

These words will be introduced after the story is read, using context from the story.

disguise   **scrumptious**   **convince**

Getting Ready for the Read-Aloud

Show children the picture on page 45 of the Hen looking at the apple tree. Read the title aloud, and tell children that the Hen in this story sees a very strange-looking apple tree in her yard!

Explain that this story is a fable, and that fables often teach a lesson, or moral, and feature animals that can talk. You may want to remind children of some fables they already know, such as *The Tortoise and the Hare.*

Ask children to listen carefully as you read the story. Challenge them to guess the moral of this fable before you read it. You might want to explain the moral as, "It is always hard to pretend to be something that you are not."

The Hen and the Apple Tree

A fable written and illustrated by Arnold Lobel

ne October day, a Hen looked out her window. She saw an apple tree growing in her backyard.

"Now that is odd," said the Hen. "I am **certain** that there was no tree standing in that spot yesterday."

"There are some of us that grow fast," said the tree.

The Hen looked at the bottom of the tree.

"I have never seen a tree," she said, "that has ten furry toes."

"There are some of us that do," said the tree. "Hen, come outside and enjoy the cool shade of my leafy branches."

Bringing the Story to Life

Use three different tones of voice as you read the Hen's dialogue, the Wolf's dialogue (the tree), and the narration. When reading the Hen's dialogue, read each statement with increasing confidence that her plan is working.

The Hen looked at the top of the tree.

"I have never seen a tree," she said, "that has two long, pointed ears."

Why does the tree look strange to the Hen?

"There are some of us that have," said the tree. "Hen, come outside and eat one of my delicious apples."

"Come to think of it," said the Hen, "I have never heard a tree speak from a mouth that is full of sharp teeth."

"There are some of us that can," said the tree. "Hen, come outside and rest your back against the bark of my trunk."

Why might the tree be asking Hen to come and rest her back against its trunk?

"I have heard," said the Hen, "that some of you trees lose all of your leaves at this time of the year."

"Oh, yes," said the tree, "there are some of us that will." The tree began to **quiver** and shake. All of its leaves quickly dropped off.

What do you think the Hen sees now?

The Hen was not surprised to see a large Wolf in the place where an apple tree had been standing just a moment before. She locked her shutters and slammed her window closed.

The Wolf knew that he had been **outsmarted**. He stormed away in a hungry rage.

It is always difficult to pose as something that one is not.

Talking About the Story

- Ask children to tell how the Hen knew the tree wasn't really a tree and how the Hen tricked the Wolf.
- Ask children whether someone has ever tried to fool them or play a trick on them. Have them describe what happened.

Vocabulary in Action

Words From the Story

certain

In the story the Hen was certain that there had been no tree in her backyard the day before. If you are certain about something, you strongly believe that it is true. Let's say *certain* together.

- Ask children which they are more certain of, their name or what the weather will be like next week. Explain.
- Ask a child to name an object that they are certain was in the classroom yesterday.

quiver

At the end of the story, the tree, which was really the Wolf, began to quiver and drop its leaves. To quiver means to shake a tiny bit. Let's say *quiver* together.

- Ask children which one can quiver, a statue or a person. Why?
- Have children act out how the Wolf might have quivered.

outsmart

The Hen knew the tree was not a tree and, in the end, outsmarted the Wolf. When you outsmart someone, you trick them or beat them by doing something clever. Let's say *outsmart* together.

- Ask children which you would be if you outsmarted someone, clever or foolish. Why?
- Have children tell what the Wolf could have done differently to outsmart the Hen.

Words About the Story

disguise

The Wolf covered himself up with branches and leaves so that he would look like an apple tree. Another way to say that is to say he put on a disguise. A disguise is something you wear to make you look like someone or something else. Let's say *disguise* together.

- Ask which is a disguise, a face mask or a backpack. Why?
- Ask a child to draw a picture of someone and then draw a disguise on the person.

scrumptious

The Wolf told the Hen that his apples were delicious. Another way to say something is delicious is to say that it is scrumptious. Something scrumptious is so delicious that you don't want to stop eating it. Let's say *scrumptious* together.

- Ask children whether when you say a food is scrumptious, you want to eat it until it is all gone or you want to throw it in the trash. Explain.
- Call on a child to pretend to eat a favorite, scrumptious food.

convince

The Wolf tried to make the Hen believe he was a tree so that she would come outside. The Wolf tried to convince the Hen that he was a tree. If you convince someone, you talk them into believing something or doing something. Let's say *convince* together.

- Ask whether it would be harder to convince a dog to get into the bath or to eat a treat. Why?
- Ask children to role-play convincing their parents to let them have a pet.

Spaghetti! Spaghetti!

In this poem a boy tells what he loves so much about his favorite food—spaghetti!

Vocabulary

Words From the Poem

These words appear in blue in the poem. You might wish to go over their meanings briefly before reading the poem.

sprinkle
When you sprinkle something, you scatter tiny pieces of it over something else.

mound
A mound of something is a big round pile.

squiggle
A squiggle is a line that bends and curves.

gobble
When you gobble food, you eat it quickly and greedily.

Words About the Poem

These words will be introduced after the poem is read, using context from the poem.

sloppy   **tribute**

Getting Ready for the Read-Aloud

Show children the picture of the boy eating a plate of spaghetti on page 50. Read the title aloud, and explain that this is a funny poem in which a boy tells why he loves spaghetti so much.

Ask children if they have ever eaten spaghetti or another kind of pasta. Invite them to share their opinions about this popular food. Ask them what kinds of toppings they like to mix with spaghetti.

Tell children that many of the words in the poem such as *wiggle, wriggle, slurpy, slishy,* and *sloshy* tell how spaghetti moves and sounds as you eat it.

Spaghetti! Spaghetti!

By Jack Prelutsky

Illustrated by Dona Turner

Spaghetti! Spaghetti!
You're wonderful stuff,
I love you, spaghetti,
I can't get enough.

You're covered with sauce
and you're **sprinkled** with cheese,
Spaghetti! Spaghetti!
Oh, give me some, please.

Spaghetti! Spaghetti!
Piled high in a **mound**,
you wiggle, you wriggle,
you **squiggle** around.

There's slurpy spaghetti
all over my plate,
Spaghetti! Spaghetti!
I think you are great.

Spaghetti! Spaghetti!
I love you a lot,
you're slishy, you're sloshy,
delicious and hot.

I **gobble** you down,
oh, I can't get enough,
Spaghetti! Spaghetti!
you're wonderful stuff.

Bringing the Poem to Life

Read the poem with exaggerated expression. Emphasize rhyming words and the words *slurpy, slishy,* and *sloshy*. When you read the phrase "Spaghetti! Spaghetti!" have children shout the words with you.

Talking About the Poem

- Ask children to talk about the different ways the boy describes spaghetti. Ask if there was a word that they especially liked or thought was funny.
- Ask children if they like spaghetti as much as the boy in the poem does. If not, have them explain why they do not like it. If so, have them describe why they like it.

Vocabulary in Action

sprinkle

In the poem the spaghetti is sprinkled with cheese. When you sprinkle something, you scatter tiny pieces of it over something else. Let's say *sprinkle* together.

- Ask which can be sprinkled, salt or a house. Why?
- Have a child show how they would sprinkle some chocolate chips on top of a cake.

mound

The spaghetti is piled high in a mound. A mound of something is a big round pile. Let's say *mound* together.

- Ask if a mound is higher or lower than the ground around it. Explain your answer.
- Have children mimic you as you use your index finger to draw the shape of a mound in the air.

squiggle

The boy in the poem says that spaghetti squiggles around. A squiggle is a line that bends and curves. Let's say *squiggle* together.

- Ask children which animal can be shaped like a squiggle, a snake or a turtle. Why?
- Call on a child to draw a line that squiggles on the board.

gobble

The boy gobbles spaghetti. When you gobble food, you eat it quickly and greedily. Let's say *gobble* together.

- Ask which you can gobble, a cookie or a T-shirt. Explain.
- Have children act out how they would gobble down a yummy sandwich.

Words About the Poem

sloppy

Spaghetti is described as a messy food to eat. Another way to say that is to say that spaghetti is a sloppy food to eat. If something is sloppy, it is messy and careless. Let's say *sloppy* together.

- Ask children which activity would be sloppier, finger painting or drawing with crayons. Why is that?
- Have children pretend that they are walking across a sloppy field where it has just rained.

tribute

This poem tells about how wonderful spaghetti is. This means the poem is a tribute to spaghetti. A tribute is something you say or do to show how important you think something or someone is. Let's say *tribute* together.

- Ask who you would make a tribute to, someone who helped you or someone who hurt your feelings. Explain your answer.
- Have children share any people they might want to make a tribute to.

The LION and the LITTLE RED BIRD

In this story a little bird finds out why a lion's tail is a new color each day.

Vocabulary

Words From the Story

These words appear in blue in the story. You might wish to go over their meanings briefly before reading the story.

wander
When you wander, you walk around as if you had no special place to go.

nibble
When you nibble food, you eat it in tiny bites.

crouch
When you crouch, you bend your knees and get down very low to the ground.

Words About the Story

These words will be introduced after the story is read, using context from the story.

artistic   inquire   patient

Getting Ready for the Read-Aloud

Show children the picture on pages 54 and 55. Read the title aloud, and tell children that this is a story about a lion and a little red bird. Ask children to point out each animal. Then point to the bird's nest and to the cave. Have children identify and tell which animal lives in each.

Explain that some stories are about real things that can really happen, and some other stories are fantasy stories about things that can't really happen. Tell children that in this story, the lion and the bird think and talk. Ask children if they think this can really happen.

The following words occur in the story. They can be briefly explained as you come to them in the story: *astonished,* surprised or amazed; *ambled,* to walk around in a slow and relaxed way; *enchanted,* extremely delighted or pleased.

The LION and the LITTLE RED BIRD

Written and illustrated by Elisa Kleven

One afternoon, a little red bird saw a lion with a bushy green tail, as green as the forest. The bird had never seen anything so unusual and so pretty. Just looking at it made her happy.

"Lion, Lion!" she said. "Why is your tail so green?" The lion didn't understand the bird's language. He thought she was simply chirping.

He smiled at her and **wandered** down to a field of orange flowers. The bird watched him roll and sniff and chase butterflies, then slowly walk west with the setting sun and disappear into a cave. The bird waited on a tree nearby. She wanted to see the lion's green tail again. But the lion did not come out of the cave, so the bird made herself a soft nest and slept through the warm starry night.

Bringing the Story to Life

Place emphasis on the color words that foreshadow the upcoming color of the lion's tail. Before revealing each new color of the lion's tail, pause to build suspense. Then announce the color with a flourish.

In the morning the lion came out, swishing his tail—which was no longer green, but orange as a flower, orange as a butterfly, orange as the setting sun.

"Lion, Lion!" the bird chirped, astonished. "Why is your tail so orange?" Again, the lion did not understand the bird.

Why do you think the lion couldn't understand what the bird was saying?

He smiled at her and climbed over the hill and up the mountain to a deep blue lake beneath a bright blue sky, where he soaked his tired paws while the bird splashed nearby.

At the end of the day the lion climbed back down the mountain, over the hill, and home to his cave. The bird settled down in the tree, wondering, as the sky darkened, about the lion and his orange tail.

But in the morning the lion's tail was no longer orange. It was blue as the brightest blue sky, blue as the deep mountain lake where he'd soaked his paws.

"Lion, Lion!" the bird chirped, enchanted. "How did your tail change from orange to blue? Are you a magician?"

The lion just smiled and ambled over to a bush full of shiny red berries. They were beautiful berries, but very sour.

"Lion," the bird chirped, making a face, "these berries are still too sour to eat! Why don't you pick them when they are ripe?"

The lion just smiled, thinking how much he liked the bird's chirping company.

All afternoon the lion picked berries while the bird **nibbled** sunflower seeds nearby. Once, when the lion stepped on a thorn, the bird pulled it out for him. At sundown, the lion swished his tail good-bye and returned to his cave. The bird settled down in her nest. She wondered what color the lion's tail would be in the morning. She wished he would answer her questions.

During the night a storm came. Thunder crashed and lightning flashed. Rain swept away the bird's nest. Hearing the noise, the lion rushed out and reached up into the tree where the bird **crouched**, shivering and scared.

He lifted her down and carried her into his cave. The cave was warm and colorful. The walls were filled with pictures of green forests, orange flowers, butterflies, sunsets, a bright blue sky, and a deep blue lake.

"Lion, Lion!" the bird chirped, delighted. "How did these pictures get here?" The lion smiled, dipped his tail into a bowl of shiny red berry juice, and painted a picture of the bird, chirping on a berry bush. The bird sang while the lion painted. She sang a song without any questions, full of color and joy.

How did the pictures get on the wall of the lion's cave?

The lion had never heard anything so unusual and so pretty. Just listening made him happy.

In the morning, the storm was past. The world shone fresh and bright. The lion's tail was berry-red, and the little bird knew why. She sang her happiest song and wondered what the lion would paint that night.

Talking About the Story

- Ask children to describe what the bird saw each day as she followed the lion.
- Ask children if they have ever wondered about something the way the bird wondered about the colors of the lion's tail. Have them describe what they wondered and how they learned the answer.

Vocabulary in Action

Words From the Story

wander

In the story the lion wandered around each day. When you wander, you walk around as if you had no special place to go. Let's say *wander* together.

- Ask children who might wander, a busy person who is on the way to an important meeting or a person on vacation who is walking on the beach. Why?
- Have children take turns wandering quietly around the classroom.

nibble

The bird nibbled sunflower seeds. When you nibble food, you eat it in tiny bites. Let's say *nibble* together.

- Ask children who might nibble, someone who is very hungry or someone who isn't very hungry. Why?
- Ask a child to pretend to be a bird nibbling on seeds.

crouch

The bird crouched in the tree after her nest was washed away in the storm. When you crouch, you bend your knees and get down very low to the ground. Let's say *crouch* together.

- Ask when you might crouch, to pick up a pencil that you dropped on the floor or to get a book off a high shelf. Explain your answer.
- Ask children to crouch as low to the ground as they can.

Words About the Story

artistic

The lion is artistic because he paints beautiful pictures on the wall of his cave. When someone is artistic, they are very good at drawing, painting, or making beautiful things. Let's say *artistic* together.

- Ask which person is artistic, someone who makes a beautiful sand castle or someone who knocks down the sand castle. Why?
- Have children be artistic and make their own pictures of the characters in the story.

inquire

The little bird asked the lion about the colors of his tail. Another way to say that is the little bird inquired about the colors of the lion's tail. When you inquire about something, you ask questions about it. Let's say *inquire* together.

- Ask which you might inquire about, a desk with nothing on it or a mysterious box with the words "Super-Secret Surprise" written on it. Explain.
- Ask children to show you what they should do in class when they want to inquire about something.

patient

All through the story, the bird asked questions and didn't get answers. But the bird never got excited or upset. The bird was always patient. When you are patient, you stay calm while you wait for something to happen. Let's say *patient* together.

- Ask children when it would be harder to be patient, when you are waiting to open presents or when you are waiting for your turn to take out the trash. Why?
- Have children tell about a time they had to be patient.

Herbert Glerbett

This fantasy poem tells about the surprising thing that happened to a boy who ate too much of his favorite food.

Vocabulary

Words From the Poem

These words appear in blue in the poem. You might wish to go over their meanings briefly before reading the poem.

dissolve
When something dissolves, it melts and disappears.

ghastly
If something is ghastly, it is the scariest thing you can think of.

sly
Someone who is sly is wise and might do things in a sneaky way to get what they want.

swift
Something that is swift moves fast.

Words About the Poem

These words will be introduced after the poem is read, using context from the poem.

preposterous   **caution**

Getting Ready for the Read-Aloud

Ask children to look at the picture of the boy melting on page 60. Read the title aloud, and have children brainstorm words to describe the boy in the picture. Point out the sherbet buckets on the floor. Be sure that children know that sherbet is a dessert similar to ice cream.

Tell children that this poem is a fantasy poem. It describes something that could never really happen, but is funny to read about.

You might wish to explain the following words and concepts as you come to them in the poem: *evolved*, changed or grew into something different; *creature*, a scary living thing.

Herbert Glerbett

By Jack Prelutsky

Illustrated by Diane Greenseid

Herbert Glerbett, rather round,
swallowed sherbet by the pound,
fifty pounds of lemon sherbet
went inside of Herbert Glerbett.

With that glop inside his lap
Herbert Glerbett took a nap,
and as he slept, the boy **dissolved**,
and from the mess a thing evolved—

a thing that is a **ghastly** green,
a thing the world had never seen,
a puddle thing, a gooey pile
of something strange that does not smile.

Now if you're wise, and if you're **sly**,
you'll **swiftly** pass this creature by,
it is no longer Herbert Glerbett.
Whatever it is, do not disturb it.

Bringing the Poem to Life

Read the first two stanzas in a lively, conversational tone. Then slow your reading and use a horrified tone to read stanza three. Read stanza four as if you are giving advice that children should take seriously.

Talking About the Poem

- Have children summarize the poem by drawing pictures of Herbert before and after his sherbet feast.
- Invite children to identify their favorite foods. Have them tell, realistically, what they think would happen if they ate too much of this food. Then encourage children to describe silly or funny things that might happen to them if they ate too much of their favorite foods.

Vocabulary in Action

Words From the Poem

dissolve

In the poem Herbert dissolved from a boy into a gooey mess. When something dissolves, it melts and disappears. Let's say *dissolve* together.

- Ask which might dissolve in the sun, an ice cube or a big, tall house. Why?
- Demonstrate for children how a spoonful of salt dissolves into a clear glass of water. Ask children to describe other things they have seen dissolve.

swift

The poet tells readers they should swiftly pass Herbert if they see him. Something that is swift moves fast. Let's say *swift* together.

- Ask which moves swiftly, a turtle or a rabbit. Explain.
- Ask children whether or not they do the following things swiftly or slowly: brush your teeth, get dressed, do your homework, pack a suitcase, run.

ghastly

Herbert turned a ghastly shade of green. If something is ghastly, it is the scariest thing you can think of. Let's say *ghastly* together.

- Ask children which would be ghastly to see on a walk in the woods, a cute squirrel or an angry bear. Explain your choice.
- Have children show how they would react if they saw Herbert turning a ghastly shade of green.

sly

The poet says that if you are sly, you will move by Herbert quickly. Someone who is sly is wise and might do things in a sneaky way to get what they want. Let's say *sly* together.

- Ask which is an example of being sly, buying cookies at a store or taking a cookie out of a cookie jar when no one is looking. Why is that?
- Move away from your desk and look in another direction. Ask a child to slyly take a pencil from your desktop, use it, and put it back.

Words About the Poem

preposterous

What happened to Herbert in the poem is unbelievable. What happened to him is preposterous. Something preposterous is so strange that it couldn't possibly be true. Let's say *preposterous* together.

- Ask children which would be preposterous, a duck that quacks or a duck that tells jokes. Why?
- Have partners tell each other a preposterous story about something they saw on the way to school.

caution

The poet tells the reader to be very careful not to get near Herbert. Another way to say that is that the poet cautions the reader to stay away from Herbert. When you caution someone, you warn that person of danger. Let's say *caution* together.

- Ask which you would caution someone about, a dollar on the ground or a slippery puddle on the ground. Explain your answer.
- Have children hold a hand in front of them, palm facing out, and shout "Caution! Look out!"

Mama Provi and the Pot of Rice

In this story Mama Provi trades rice with chicken for other kinds of food and is able to bring her sick granddaughter Lucy a wonderful feast.

Vocabulary

Words From the Story

These words appear in blue in the story. You might wish to go over their meanings briefly before reading the story.

tremendous

If something is tremendous, it is very large or in a very large amount.

amazed

If something has amazed you, it has surprised you very much.

rearrange

If you rearrange things, you change the way in which they are organized or ordered.

sliver

A sliver of something is a small, thin piece of it.

Words About the Story

These words will be introduced after the story is read, using context from the story.

palate   **surplus**

Getting Ready for the Read-Aloud

Show children the picture on page 64 of Mama Provi walking up the stairs in her apartment building. Read the title aloud and explain to children that in this story, Mama Provi is bringing food to her granddaughter, Lucy, who is sick with the chicken pox.

Explain that Mama Provi grew up in Puerto Rico. Use a map or globe to show Puerto Rico's location in relation to where the children are. Tell children that people in Puerto Rico speak Spanish and that several Spanish words are used in this story.

You might wish to explain that *chicken pox* is a mild disease that causes a rash, or small red spots, on the skin.

Mama Provi
and the
Pot of Rice

By Sylvia Rosa-Casanova
Illustrated by Robert Roth

M

Mama Provi lived on the first floor of a tall apartment building. Her granddaughter, Lucy, who was six years old, lived with her parents on the eighth floor of the very same building.

Twice a month, Lucy spent the night at Mama Provi's. They played games and listened to old, scratchy records. At bedtime, Lucy always begged Mama Provi for a story. Mama Provi wove marvelous tales about when she was a little girl growing up in Puerto Rico with her five brothers and four sisters. Lucy fell asleep to stories filled with palm trees, sweet mangoes, and tiny tree frogs called *coquís* (koh KEES).

In the morning, Lucy helped Mama Provi cook breakfast. It was always a **tremendous** feast because Mama Provi didn't know how to cook for only two people. In her big family, she had been taught to cook for a dozen people at one time.

One Saturday, Lucy's mama called to say that Lucy had the chicken pox and would not be able to visit that evening. Lucy was very sad. Mama Provi wondered what she could do to cheer her up.

Before long, Mama Provi had a wonderful idea. Lucy always said that Mama Provi made the best rice with chicken in the whole world. And so, Mama Provi took out her largest pot and set out to make the most delicious *arroz con pollo* (ah ROHS KOHN POH yoh) ever.

Bringing the Story to Life

Draw on the board an apartment building with eight floors. After you read the first paragraph, write *Mama Provi* on the first floor and *Lucy* on the eighth floor. As you read, trace Mama Provi's route and act out her knocking.

Why do you think Mama Provi is making rice with chicken?

When the rice had cooled just enough, Mama Provi packed the pot in an enormous shopping bag. She locked her door and started up the stairs to the eighth floor. Mama Provi never, ever rode the elevator.

The pot of rice was heavy and it was not long before Mama Provi had to stop to catch her breath. She was resting on the second floor landing when a wondrous smell tickled her nose. She recognized the aroma instantly and without giving it another thought, knocked briskly on apartment 2B.

Mrs. Landers opened the door.

"Excuse me for bothering you, Mrs. Landers, but is that your crusty white bread that I smell?" Mama Provi asked.

Mrs. Landers said it was.

"I wonder if you would trade a bit of your bread for a bowl of my *arroz con pollo*. I am taking this rice to Lucy, who is sick with the chicken pox, and a piece of your bread would go so well with it."

Mrs. Landers was only too pleased to make the trade for she also loved Mama Provi's *arroz con pollo*. *En un dos por tres* (EHN OON DOHS POHR TREHS), which in Spanish means something like "lickedy-split," Mrs. Landers wrapped up a large chunk of her freshly baked bread and exchanged it for a bowl of Mama Provi's rice.

After thanking Mrs. Landers, Mama Provi continued up the stairs carrying the pot of rice and the chunk of bread.

Mama Provi had not gone very far when she again stopped to catch her breath, this time on the third floor. Again a delightful smell tickled her nose. She recognized the aroma instantly and without giving it another thought, knocked briskly on apartment 3E.

Señor Rivera answered the door.

"Excuse me for bothering you, Señor Rivera, but are those your *frijoles negros* (free HOH lehs NEH grohs) that I smell?" Mama Provi asked.

Señor Rivera said they were.

"I wonder if you would trade a bit of your black beans for a bowl of the *arroz con pollo* I have in this pot. I am taking this rice to Lucy, who is sick with the chicken pox, and your beans would go so well with the rice."

Señor Rivera was only too pleased to make the trade. *En un dos por tres,* he poured a generous helping of his beans into a container and exchanged it for a bowl of Mama Provi's rice.

What food besides rice with chicken is Mama Provi carrying now?

When Mama Provi reached the fourth floor, she was surprised to find Mrs. Bazzini from apartment 4G waiting for her.

"Mrs. Landers called to tell me that you have a large pot of *arroz con pollo* that you are taking to Lucy," said Mrs. Bazzini. "I was wondering if you would trade a bowl for some of my fresh green salad."

Mama Provi agreed immediately. A nice tossed salad would indeed go very well with her *arroz con pollo*. So, *en un dos por tres*, Mrs. Bazzini exchanged a bowl of salad for a bowl of Mama Provi's rice.

After thanking Mrs. Bazzini, Mama Provi continued up the stairs carrying the pot of rice, the chunk of bread, the container of black beans, and the bowl of salad.

Having given away so much of her rice, Mama Provi was **amazed** that her shopping bag was still so heavy. She was resting on the fifth floor when a heavenly smell tickled her nose. She recognized the aroma instantly and knocked briskly on apartment 5A.

> Why is Mama Provi's shopping bag still so heavy even though she has given away so much of her rice?

Mrs. Johnson opened the door.

"Excuse me for bothering you, Mrs. Johnson, but are those your collard greens that I smell?" Mama Provi asked.

Mrs. Johnson said they were.

"I wonder if you could trade a bit of those greens for a bowl of the *arroz con pollo* I have in this pot. I am taking this rice to Lucy, who is sick with the chicken pox, and your collard greens would go so well with the rice."

En un dos por tres, Mrs. Johnson wrapped up a generous portion of her collard greens and exchanged it for a bowl of Mama Provi's rice.

> What does Mama Provi have in her shopping bag now?

When Mama Provi reached the sixth floor, she bumped straight into Mrs. Woo.

"Mrs. Bazzini called to say that Lucy is ill with the chicken pox," said Mrs. Woo. "Please take this tea to her. I hope it will make her feel better."

Mama Provi asked Mrs. Woo if she would like a bowl of *arroz con pollo* but Mrs. Woo said she would wait until the next time Mama Provi made her tasty rice.

After thanking Mrs. Woo, Mama Provi continued up the stairs carrying the pot of rice, the chunk of bread, the container of black beans, the bowl of salad, the generous portion of collard greens, and the pot of tea.

On the seventh floor, Mama Provi stopped to **rearrange** her shopping bag. Another enchanting smell tickled her nose. She recognized it instantly and knocked briskly on apartment 7C.

Mrs. Kelly answered the door.

"Excuse me for bothering you, Mrs. Kelly, but is that your apple pie that I smell?" Mama Provi asked.

Mrs. Kelly said it was.

"I wonder if you would trade a **sliver** of your delicious apple pie for a bowl of the *arroz con pollo* I have in this pot. I am taking this rice to Lucy, who is sick with the chicken pox, and your apple pie would make such a nice dessert.

Mrs. Kelly was only too pleased to make the trade and she exchanged a healthy slice of her apple pie for a bowl of Mama Provi's rice.

How big do you think a healthy slice of apple pie is?

Although Mama Provi had given away quite a bit of her *arroz con pollo,* her shopping bag was still very heavy. She had finally reached the eighth floor and had stopped to catch her breath when a delicious, heavenly, enchanting, wondrous, delightful odor tickled her nose. It was her *arroz con pollo,* Mrs. Landers's freshly baked bread, Señor Rivera's black beans, Mrs. Bazzini's green salad, Mrs. Johnson's collard greens, Mrs. Woo's tea, and Mrs. Kelly's apple pie. Without giving it another thought, she knocked briskly on apartment 8F.

How did Mama Provi end up with so much food?

Lucy answered the door. She was covered with spots.

"Excuse me for bothering you, but are you the little girl who is sick with the chicken pox and cannot come to visit her grandmother?"

Lucy said she was and then hugged Mama Provi as hard as she could.

Mama Provi pointed to the enormous shopping bag. Together they carried it into the apartment and, *en un dos por tres,* they set up a tremendous feast.

"Let's eat!" said Mama Provi.

And that's exactly what they did.

Talking About the Story

- Ask children to recall the different foods that Mama Provi received from her neighbors in exchange for some of her rice with chicken.

- Invite children to talk about a relative with whom they have a special relationship, just as Lucy had with her grandmother. Have children tell why they enjoy spending time with that person.

Vocabulary in Action

tremendous

In the story Mama Provi always cooked a tremendous feast for breakfast. If something is tremendous, it is very large or in a very large amount. Let's say *tremendous* together.

- Ask which is tremendous, a bathtub or a huge swimming pool. Why?
- Ask children to show how they would look carrying a bowl filled with a tremendous amount of spaghetti.

amazed

Mama Provi was amazed that her shopping bag was still so heavy after she gave away so much of her rice with chicken. If something has amazed you, it has surprised you very much. Let's say *amazed* together.

- Ask children which would amaze them, if a child walked into the classroom or if a child flew into the classroom. Explain.
- Ask children to discuss what things they have seen that amazed them.

rearrange

Mama Provi stopped to rearrange her shopping bag after receiving food from her neighbors. If you rearrange things, you change the way in which they are organized or ordered. Let's say *rearrange* together.

- Ask which you might rearrange, a drawer full of spoons and forks all mixed up together or a drawer full of neatly folded socks. Why is that?
- Have children help you rearrange some part of the classroom.

sliver

Mama Provi asked Mrs. Kelly if she would trade a sliver of her apple pie for a bowl of rice with chicken. A sliver of something is a small, thin piece of it. Let's say *sliver* together.

- Ask children to tell when they would want a sliver of chocolate cake, when they were almost full or when they were really hungry. Explain.
- Have children take a piece of paper and cut a few slivers of paper from it.

Words About the Story

palate

In the story Mama Provi liked many different foods. This means that many different foods pleased Mama Provi's palate. Someone's palate is their choice of what foods and drinks they like. Let's say *palate* together.

- Ask children if a food pleased their palate, would they say that the food was terrible or that it was tasty. Explain.
- Ask children to draw a picture of a food that pleases their palate.

surplus

Mama Provi always cooked more food than she needed. Another way to say that is to say Mama Provi always cooked a surplus of food. You have a surplus of something when you have more than you need of it. Let's say *surplus* together.

- Ask children which is a surplus of rain, when the flowers in your garden are getting just enough water or when your home is flooding with water. Why?
- Give two children a pencil each and a third child two pencils. Ask children to tell you which child has a surplus of pencils and why.

Never Trust a SQUIRREL

In this story a guinea pig named William learns that he can't trust squirrels, but he can always trust his mother.

Vocabulary

Words From the Story

These words appear in blue in the story. You might wish to go over their meanings briefly before reading the story.

dull
If you say something is dull, you mean that it is rather boring and not very exciting.

eager
If you are eager for something, you want it so much you can hardly wait.

alert
If you alert someone, you make them aware of something that is important or dangerous.

Words About the Story

These words will be introduced after the story is read, using context from the story.

petrified   **adventurous**   **rely**

Getting Ready for the Read-Aloud

Show children the picture on pages 72 and 73 of the squirrel and guinea pig. Read the title aloud, and tell children that in this story, a little guinea pig learns that he can't trust a squirrel.

Tell children that a guinea pig belongs to the same animal family as mice, woodchucks, and squirrels. Point out that a guinea pig has short ears, short legs, and a very short tail.

You might wish to explain the following words and concepts as you come to them in the story. Explain that a *hutch* is a pen or coop for small animals. A *pellet* is a little ball of food. Things *scamper* when they run very quickly. When something *scrabbles*, it digs around or scratches with its nails or claws. When you *dislodge* something, you unstick it from where it was before.

By Patrick Cooper
Illustrated by Catherine Walters

Never Trust a SQUIRREL

 t was a beautiful day, and William the guinea pig was bored. He sat staring out of his hutch, wondering what to do next.

He thought about asking his mother for ideas, but he knew what she would say: "Play a game of hide-the-pellet" or "Chew on some hay." His mother could always find things to do, but they were **dull**, guinea-pig things.

William sighed. He was just about to close his eyes for a nap when, suddenly, a squirrel dropped out of the nut tree and looked in at him.

"Hiya," said the squirrel. "I'm Stella. Who are you?"

"William," said William hopefully. Maybe Stella would invite him to play. Squirrels seemed to have a lot of fun chasing one another around the yard and chattering in the trees.

Sure enough, Stella said, "Well, William, I'm going exploring. Want to come?"

But before he could answer, she scampered back up the branch and across the treetops.

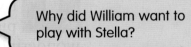

Bringing the Story to Life

Use pantomime to act out the many physical parts of this story, such as hiding in a drainpipe, trying to climb a tree, and trying to dislodge the hiding guinea pigs. Read the section at the top of page 76 with heightened suspense.

> Why did William want to play with Stella?

"Wait," said William, but she was gone. And he couldn't run into the yard to look for her, because he wasn't allowed out of the hutch without his mother.

Being a guinea pig was hard, but being a young guinea pig was worse.

William watched for Stella until bedtime, but there was no sign of his new friend.

That night his mother promised, "We'll go for a long walk tomorrow, William. You'll like that."

But William had other plans....

The next day, Stella appeared at their door.

"Come into the woods and play," she chittered.

"I can't get out," said William sadly. "The door is locked."

"I'll fix that," said Stella, and she nibbled off the catch.

"William," cried his mother, "stay here. The woods aren't safe for guinea pigs."

But William didn't listen.

Why didn't William listen to his mother?

The two adventurers reached the cool shade of the trees.

"Let's climb!" Stella suggested. She scampered up a tree trunk.

"Okay," said William **eagerly**. He made a running start, grabbed at the bark with his tiny paws, and rolled back into the grass. Guinea pigs can't climb.

"Silly old guinea pig," said Stella, laughing.

"I can play hide-and-seek," offered William.

William hid in a piece of old drainpipe. He stayed very still, and Stella couldn't find him.

"I give up!" said Stella crossly. She liked to win every game. "This is stupid. Let's play chase instead."

William chased Stella down the hill. He was having so much fun that he didn't hear the blackbird at first.

"Run! Run!" it squawked. "Fox! Run, run!"

William was terrified.

"Wh-what do we do now?" he stammered.

"Easy," said Stella. "We just run up a tree."

"But I can't climb!" wailed William.

"Oh, right," said Stella. "That's too bad. Well, I'll see you later."

Was Stella a good friend to William? Why or why not?

And the squirrel was gone again.

"Fox! Fox!" called the blackbird. "Hide, guinea pig, hide!"

But where? William looked around wildly, then dived under some low branches and fallen leaves.

He stayed very still, hoping the fox was no better at searching than Stella.

The leaves quivered. William saw a black nose and sharp, pointed teeth. He felt the fox's warm breath as it rooted through the leaves.

William buried himself deeper, but the movement **alerted** the fox. It gave a yelp of excitement and scrabbled at the leaf pile.

THUD!

The fox jumped back as the drainpipe came thumping down the hill. Behind it came William's mother. The pipe rolled to a stop near William. "Quick!" called his mother. "Get in!" The frightened guinea pig darted into one end of the pipe. His mother rushed into the other.

She held him close as the fox poked its nose into the pipe. It tried one end, then it tried the other end. It shook the pipe and rolled it, trying to dislodge the little guinea pigs. But William and his mother stayed deep inside, huddled together.

And then the fox gave up. William and his mother waited inside the pipe just to be sure. At last the blackbird sang, "All clear! The fox is gone." William's mother peeked out of the pipe and said, "It's time to go home, little one."

> How did William's mother protect both of them from the fox?

William raced back to the hutch and hid in the straw. He was sure his mother was angry with him. But when she spoke, her voice was soft. "William, I'll take you exploring tomorrow. And if you learn to be careful, someday you can go alone. But you must listen to me from now on.

"And William," she added, "never trust a squirrel."

"Okay," William squeaked.

And he didn't.

Talking About the Story

- Ask children to explain why William could not trust Stella. Have them tell which character William could always trust.
- Invite children to talk about people they trust and need. Have children explain why they trust them.

Vocabulary in Action

dull

In the story William was tired of doing dull, guinea-pig things. If you say something is dull, you mean that it is rather boring and not very exciting. Let's say *dull* together.

- Ask which is dull, waiting in line or riding a roller coaster. Why?
- Ask children to show how they would look if they were listening to someone tell a dull story.

eager

William is eager to follow Stella and climb a tree. If you are eager for something, you want it so much you can hardly wait. Let's say *eager* together.

- Ask which would you be eager to do, eat a wonderful dinner or wash all the dishes afterwards. Explain.
- Ask a child to show how a person who is eager to get called on might act.

alert

William's movements under the branches alerted the fox that someone was there. If you alert someone, you make them aware of something important or dangerous. Let's say *alert* together.

- Ask children if they would alert someone if they saw smoke coming out of an oven. Why or why not?
- Have a child tell about a time that someone alerted them of something important.

Words About the Story

petrified

In the story William was very scared when the fox came after him. You could even say William was petrified. If you are petrified, you are so scared that you can hardly move. Let's say *petrified* together.

- Ask which might make you petrified, finding a cat in your backyard or a lion in your bed. Explain your answer.
- Ask children to show how petrified they would look if a bear walked into the classroom.

adventurous

Stella liked to explore and try new things. Another way to say that is to say Stella was adventurous. Someone who is adventurous is willing to take risks and to try new things. Let's say *adventurous* together.

- Ask which would be adventurous, someone painting a picture of a mountain or someone climbing a mountain. Why?
- Call on a child to tell about a book or movie that told an adventurous story.

rely

Stella left William behind and didn't help him at all when the fox came. William could not rely on Stella. When you rely on someone, you count on them to do something for you. Let's say *rely* together.

- Ask whether someone you rely on would remember to pack your lunch or forget to cook you dinner. Explain.
- Ask children to name people they rely on every day.

Flip-Flops

This story tells how a girl started with a problem and ended up with a new friend.

Vocabulary

Words From the Story

These words appear in blue in the story. You might wish to go over their meanings briefly before reading the story.

relax
When you relax, you let go of all your worries and you rest.

appear
When someone or something appears, you are suddenly able to see it.

tumble
When you tumble, you fall head first and roll over into a ball.

Words About the Story

These words will be introduced after the story is read, using context from the story.

leisure   **resourceful**   **outgoing**

Getting Ready for the Read-Aloud

Ask children to look at the picture on page 79. Read the title aloud. Encourage children to predict where the story takes place. Have them tell how they know.

Point out the shoe in the top section of the picture. Be sure children know that this kind of sandal is called a flip-flop. Invite children who have flip-flops to describe them and tell where they wear these shoes.

You might wish to explain the following words and concepts as you come to them in the story: *fanning*, waving something flat back and forth to make a cool breeze; *hermit crab*, a crab that crawls inside an empty shell of another animal and uses it to protect its body. Also explain that the phrase *happy as clams* means "very happy."

Flip-Flops

Written and illustrated by Nancy Cote

ama lifted the shade in Penny's bedroom window. The sun poured in.

"Can Penny come out to play?" called Charlotte from outside.

"Not today," Mama answered. "Today is our beach day!"

Penny had forgotten that it was Mama's day off. She'd forgotten about the beach. She jumped out of bed and watched Charlotte join some girls playing double dutch.

What could she do? Mama was already packing the car.

After breakfast, Penny squeezed into last year's bathing suit and looked for her flip-flops. She could only find one.

"What good is this?" she complained.

Mama helped Penny search, but the missing flip-flop was nowhere to be found. So Penny hopped with one flop all the way to the car.

> What is Penny's problem?

First they rode through the city, then over a bridge and past a dairy farm. Penny knew they were close when they came to the stand that sold towels and beachballs, candy and pops, shovels and pails, and pairs of flip-flops. She crossed her fingers, hoping Mama would pull over.

"Look!" cried Mama. "I can see the ocean!"

And the car rolled on.

Soon they were at the beach.

Bringing the Story to Life

As you read the story, use a real flip-flop or one made from paper to act out how Penny uses her flip-flop. Then have pairs of children use construction paper to make flip-flops and act out how Meggie and Penny became friends.

Mama sat down to **relax**. Penny wished she could find someone to play with.

A woman sitting nearby was fanning herself. Penny didn't have a fan. All she had was a flip-flop. She took it off and waved it back and forth.

The woman winked at Penny.

"Do you have any children here today?" Penny asked her.

"I have two granddaughters just about your age, but they're away at camp," she said.

"I bet they're having fun," thought Penny.

By the water, she saw a girl building a sand castle. Penny didn't have a shovel, but she did have a flip-flop. She plopped down alongside the girl and began digging. The girl smiled at Penny.

But suddenly, her big brother **appeared** and carried his giggling sister off for a swim.

> Do you think Penny is having fun at the beach? Why or why not?

At the shore, some boys were sailing toy boats. Penny didn't have a boat, but she did have a flip-flop. She joined the boys and won two out of three races!

Soon the boys were hungry. They gave Penny a high-five and raced home for lunch.

Penny sighed.

"Want to catch hermit crabs?" she heard someone ask. Penny turned around.

"My name is Meggie," said a girl. "Are you afraid of crabs? I like them, but I'm afraid to pick them up."

"Me, too," agreed Penny, "but I have an idea."

> What do you think Penny's idea is?

She bent her flip-flop in half like a crab claw. Then she scooped up crabs and sand, and in no time she and Meggie had filled half a bucket without touching even one crab.

"You have great ideas!" Meggie said.

"I have a better idea," said Penny. "Let's be friends!"

Meggie did a back flip. Penny tried to flip but flopped onto the sand.

Meggie showed Penny how to roll, **tumble**, and spin across the beach.

That afternoon, with Penny's flip-flop, they played catch, chased sea gulls, rescued stranded starfish from the hot sun...

and wrote a special message in the sand. Friends Forever.

Is Penny having fun now? Tell why.

Together, they made a perfect pair.

When it was time to go, Penny wrote Meggie's phone number on the flip-flop and promised to call.

On their way home, Penny and Mama came to the stand that sold towels and beachballs, candy and pops, shovels and pails, and pairs of flip-flops.

Mama pulled the car over. "Would you like to get something here, Penny?" she asked.

Looking at her flip-flop, Penny smiled. "No thanks, Mama. I have everything I need."

"Me, too," Mama agreed.

And off they went, happy as clams.

Talking About the Story

- Have children summarize the story by drawing each event that happened on the beach on a separate sheet of paper and then putting the events in order.
- Encourage children to tell about a time they lost something. Ask them to explain how they found the thing or how they managed without it.

Vocabulary in Action

relax

In the story Mama relaxed on the beach. When you relax, you let go of all your worries and you rest. Let's say *relax* together.

- Ask who is relaxing, someone who is sleeping in a hammock or someone who is running to catch a plane. Tell why.
- Have children act out relaxing at their desks.

appear

A little girl's brother appeared while the girl was playing with Penny. When someone or something appears, you are suddenly able to see it. Let's say *appear* together.

- Ask children who is appearing, someone jumping out from behind a tree or someone climbing a tree. Explain your answer.
- Have two volunteers go into the hall where they can't be seen from the classroom. Then ask them to appear at the door.

tumble

Meggie showed Penny how to tumble. When you tumble, you fall head first and roll over into a ball. You can either tumble on purpose or as an accident. Let's say *tumble* together.

- Ask who might tumble, someone running over bumpy ground or someone standing next to a wall. Why is that?
- Ask a volunteer to slowly tumble on a soft carpet or mat.

Words About the Story

leisure

In the story Mama likes to go to the beach when she isn't working. That means she likes to spend her leisure time at the beach. Leisure is time you have to just do what you enjoy. Let's say *leisure* together.

- Ask which time is leisure time, Monday morning when you are going to school or Saturday afternoon when you have nothing planned to do. Explain your choice.
- Ask children to describe what they do during their leisure time.

resourceful

Penny finds many ways to use her one flip-flop. Another way to say that is that Penny is very resourceful. Someone who is resourceful is good at finding ways of solving problems. Let's say *resourceful* together.

- Ask who is resourceful, someone who stands out in the rain and gets wet or who puts a jacket over their head to stay dry. Why?
- Have children discuss some times when they have been resourceful when solving a problem.

outgoing

Penny talks to and plays with many different people. Another way to say that is that Penny is very outgoing. An outgoing person is very friendly and likes to meet people. Let's say *outgoing* together.

- Ask what an outgoing person would do if they saw a person they didn't know, say hello to the person or hide behind a table. Explain.
- Ask children to talk about whether they are outgoing when meeting someone new or not.

My Building

This poem describes how interesting life can be when you live in a tall building full of people.

Vocabulary

Words From the Poem

These words appear in blue in the poem. You might wish to go over their meanings briefly before reading the poem.

glimpse
To get a glimpse of something means to get a quick look at it.

pleasant
Something pleasant is very nice and it pleases you.

strain
To strain means to push, pull, or stretch something in a way that might hurt it.

grand
If you say something is grand, you think it is so wonderful that you almost can't believe it is real.

Words About the Poem

These words will be introduced after the poem is read, using context from the poem.

skyscraper   **observant**

Getting Ready for the Read-Aloud

Show children the picture of the apartment building on page 85. Read the title aloud, and explain that this poem is about a tall apartment building. Tell children that this poem has rhyming words that describe the many people and things one boy sees in his building.

Explain that in an apartment building a different person or family lives in separate apartments inside the building. Many different people can live in one apartment building.

As you come to these words in the poem, give the following brief explanations: *nannies*, people who take care of children; *super*, a person who takes care of a building and fixes things; *doorman*, a man who opens the door and accepts packages for people who live in a building.

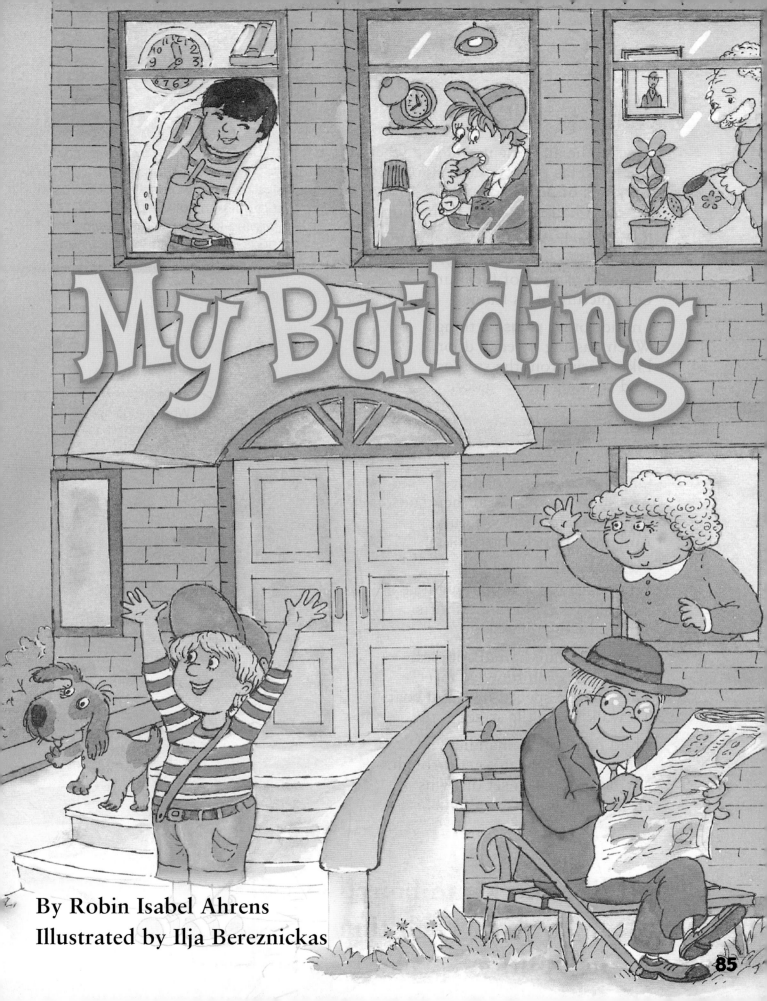

My Building

By Robin Isabel Ahrens

Illustrated by Ilja Bereznickas

The apartment building where I live
Has twenty-seven floors.
All kinds of people come and go
Through hallways lined with doors.

Behind each door there is a home,
And no two look the same.
I catch a **glimpse** of furniture
Or a picture in its frame.

I notice other **pleasant** things
When passing by each door,
Like music from the stereos
And cooking smells galore.

As you read this poem, emphasize the rhyming words. Use gestures to act out parts of the poem, such as waving to the children, petting the dogs, and saluting the doorman.

What things does the boy notice in his building?

On weekdays I see daddies
And some mommies in their suits,
A policeman who's off duty
And a man in cowboy boots!

I wave to all the children
Who leave for school at eight,
And older kids in fancy shorts
Who bike or roller skate.

I like the white-haired couples,
Who smile each time we meet.
They put on special hats and coats
To walk along the street.

I find help for the nannies
Whose strollers can't get through.
My favorite has a set of twins
Dressed up in pink and blue.

I pet the dogs both tall and small
Who exercise each day.
They bark and **strain** their leashes
As they rush outside to play.

Deliverymen march through the halls,
With things that look so **grand**,
Like flowers wrapped in cellophane
Or food from every land.

They all chat with the super,
Whose keys go *clink-clink-clink!*
He brings a big red toolbox
When he comes to fix our sink.

The mailman nods and winks at me
When he stops by at ten.
He fills the boxes one by one,
Then locks them up again.

Who are some of the
people the boy sees in
his building?

I salute the smiling doorman
In his uniform so neat.
He wishes me, "Good day! Have fun!"
And leads me to the street.

From there I see my building,
Which almost scrapes the sky.
I'm glad to be a part of it—
Not just a passerby.

Talking About the Poem

- Ask children to recall all the people and things the boy sees in his apartment building. Then ask why they think the boy is happy living in the building.

- Ask children if they would like to live in a tall building with lots of people. Have them explain why they feel as they do.

Vocabulary in Action

glimpse

In the poem the boy catches a glimpse of the furniture and pictures in other people's apartments. To get a glimpse of something means to get a quick look at it. Let's say *glimpse* together.

- Would you be more likely to glimpse at your own book or at a book someone next to you is reading? Explain.
- Have a few children act out glimpsing at different things in the room.

strain

The poem describes dogs that strain their leashes. To strain means to push, pull, or stretch something in a way that might hurt it. Let's say *strain* together.

- Ask children if they strain to close a door, is it easy or hard to close. Why?
- Have children act out how they would strain at a rope if they were having a tug-of-war.

pleasant

The boy notices some pleasant things while passing by the doors of different apartments. Something pleasant is very nice and it pleases you. Let's say *pleasant* together.

- Ask children what kind of weather they think is pleasant, warm sunny weather or cold rainy weather. Explain your choice.
- Call on volunteers to describe their most pleasant day.

grand

The boy sees deliverymen walk through the halls with things that look grand. If you say something is grand, you think it is so wonderful that you almost can't believe it is real. Let's say *grand* together.

- Ask children which kind of food is more likely to be grand, a peanut butter sandwich or a fancy cake. Tell why.
- Have children act out how they would walk down the street if they were wearing something grand, like a cape and a crown.

Words About the Poem

skyscraper

In the poem the boy lives in a tall apartment building. The boy even describes the building as almost scraping the sky. Another word for a tall building is a skyscraper. A skyscraper is a very tall building in a city. Let's say *skyscraper* together.

- Ask children if they think that there are more light switches in a skyscraper or a house. Explain your answer.
- Ask children to pretend they are in a city, looking up at all the skyscrapers around them.

observant

The boy pays attention to all the things that go on in the building. Another way to say that is to say he is observant. Someone who is observant pays a lot of attention to things. Let's say *observant* together.

- Ask children if an observant person might remember or forget what you were wearing yesterday. Why?
- Ask children to name some things an observant person might notice while walking through the park.

RABBIT COUNTS THE CROCODILES

In this Japanese legend, Rabbit tricks Crocodile and his family, but Rabbit ends up paying for his trick by losing his tail!

Vocabulary

Words From the Story

These words appear in blue in the story. You might wish to go over their meanings briefly before reading the story.

longs

When someone longs for something, they want it very badly, but think they will never have it.

realize

If you realize something, you begin to understand it or figure it out.

furious

To be furious is to be very, very mad.

admit

If you admit something, you agree that it is true, even though you may not want to have to say it.

Words About the Story

These words will be introduced after the story is read, using context from the story.

cunning   **gullible**

Getting Ready for the Read-Aloud

Show children the picture on pages 90 and 91 of Rabbit and Crocodile. Read the title aloud, and tell children that in this story, Rabbit wants to cross the sea and thinks that Crocodile may be able to help him.

Tell children that this story is a legend, and that a legend is a popular story handed down from the past. Some legends explain why a thing is the way it is.

Explain to children that the *mainland* is the main part of a country, which is separate from its islands. You may want to use a map or globe to point out the mainland of Japan and the Okinawa Islands.

RABBIT COUNTS THE CROCODILES

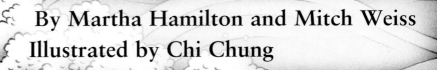

By Martha Hamilton and Mitch Weiss

Illustrated by Chi Chung

68

Long ago, Rabbit had a fine, long, bushy tail like a raccoon's. Back then, just as now, he was always up to one kind of trick or another. It was one of his tricks that caused him to lose his long tail. Let me tell you how it happened.

Rabbit lived on the island of Oki, (OH kee) just off the coast of Japan. Although he had a good life, Rabbit **longed** to see what it was like on the mainland. He would spend hours staring across the sea, wishing he knew how to swim.

Bringing the Story to Life

When Rabbit speaks at the beginning of the story, emphasize the word *hundred*. In Crocodile's response, emphasize *hundreds* and *thousands*. At the end of the story, open your arms wide and snap them together to show what the last crocodile did!

How would being able to swim help Rabbit?

One day when Crocodile swam near the shore, an idea came to Rabbit. He called out, "Crocodile, do you **realize** I have *hundreds* of rabbits in my family. It's a shame you have so few crocodiles in yours."

"Who told you that?" snapped Crocodile. "Why, there are hundreds, maybe even thousands, of crocodiles in my family!"

This reaction was just what Rabbit had hoped for. "So far, so good," Rabbit thought to himself. "My plan just might work." Then he said to Crocodile, "Well, if there are so many in your family, how come I only see one of you now and then?"

What do you think Rabbit's plan is?

"That's easy," replied Crocodile. "Because we're usually hidden below the water."

"Well, I won't believe it until I see it. Why don't you call all your crocodile family here so I can count them?"

Crocodile was **furious**. She shouted, "Fine, you little ball of fur, you stay right here. I'll show you just how many crocodiles are in my family." Crocodile then dove under the water and disappeared.

Soon many crocodiles began to appear. Before long, there were hundreds and hundreds of crocodiles swimming toward the island.

Rabbit then said to Crocodile, "I must **admit** that you have a lot of crocodiles in your family. But I can't count them when they're in a big clump like this. Tell them to get in a long line."

> Do you think Rabbit really wants to count the crocodiles? Why or why not?

The crocodiles made one long, straight line that stretched all the way to the mainland. Rabbit began to hop across the backs of the crocodiles. As he did, he counted, "One, two, three, four, five…" and on and on until he was almost to the mainland.

When he was just about to step on the last crocodile, he couldn't keep from laughing and shouting, "Oh foolish crocodiles, thanks so much for making a bridge for me!"

When the last crocodile heard this, she opened her jaws wide to eat Rabbit. But all she managed to bite off was Rabbit's tail. That's why, to this day, all rabbits have short tails.

Talking About the Story

- Ask children what Rabbit did to trick Crocodile and her family. Have them also talk about the mistake Rabbit made at the end.
- Ask children if anyone has ever tried to trick them. Have them describe what happened.

Vocabulary in Action

longs

In the story Rabbit longs to go to the mainland. When someone longs for something, they want it very badly, but think they will never have it. Let's say *longs* together.

- Ask children which one they would long for, staying up late or going to bed. Why?
- Have a child show how Rabbit might have looked as she longed to be on the mainland.

furious

Crocodile is furious with Rabbit. To be furious is to be very, very mad. Let's say *furious* together.

- Ask which would make you furious, someone giving you a bike or someone taking your bike away. Explain your answer.
- Have a child show how Crocodile might have acted when he was furious with Rabbit.

realize

Rabbit asks Crocodile if she realizes that there are hundreds of rabbits in his family. If you realize something, you begin to understand it or figure it out. Let's say *realize* together.

- Ask children how they might realize that someone had tricked them. Explain.
- Have children act like someone who realizes they can answer a question.

admit

Rabbit admits that Crocodile has a big family. If you admit something, you agree that it is true, even though you may not want to have to say it. Let's say *admit* together.

- Ask children whether they think it is easy or hard to admit something. Why?
- Have children act out how they would admit they were wrong about something.

Words About the Story

cunning

Rabbit tricks Crocodile into helping him get to the mainland. Another way to say that is to say Rabbit is cunning. If you are cunning, you are able to trick people. Let's say *cunning* together.

- Ask which might a cunning person do, tell the truth or lie. Why?
- Ask children to act out what a cunning person might do if they didn't want anyone else to know they were in the room.

gullible

Crocodile is easily tricked by Rabbit. In other words, Crocodile is gullible. Someone who is gullible is easily tricked because they believe whatever they are told. Let's say *gullible* together.

- Ask if a gullible person would believe someone who told them the sky was falling. Why?
- Ask children to show how a gullible character might act if someone said the sky was falling.

MICKEY MOUSE SPEAKS!

People all over the world know Mickey Mouse, but do you know how the cartoon Mickey began? Here is a true story about the first Mickey Mouse cartoons.

Vocabulary

Words From the Story

These words appear in blue in the story. You might wish to go over their meanings briefly before reading the story.

romp
When children or animals romp, they play happily.

fad
If something is a fad, it is popular for a very short time.

gather
When you gather things, you collect them all into a group.

household
Your household is your home, all of the people who live there, and all of the things that are a part of it.

Words About the Story

These words will be introduced after the story is read, using context from the story.

entertain   **creative**

Getting Ready for the Read-Aloud

Show children the photo on page 96 of Walt Disney and explain that he created the character Mickey Mouse. Read the title aloud, and invite children to tell what they know about Mickey Mouse.

Explain that before people had televisions, they went to the movies to see stories and cartoons. The first movies were silent—they had no sound. There were signs on the screen that people had to read to see what the characters were saying. This story tells about what happened when people first began to make movies with sound.

These words appear in the story. Explain them briefly as you come to them: *merry*, happy; *vague*, not very clear; *movie business*, all the people involved in making movies.

MICKEY MOUSE SPEAKS!

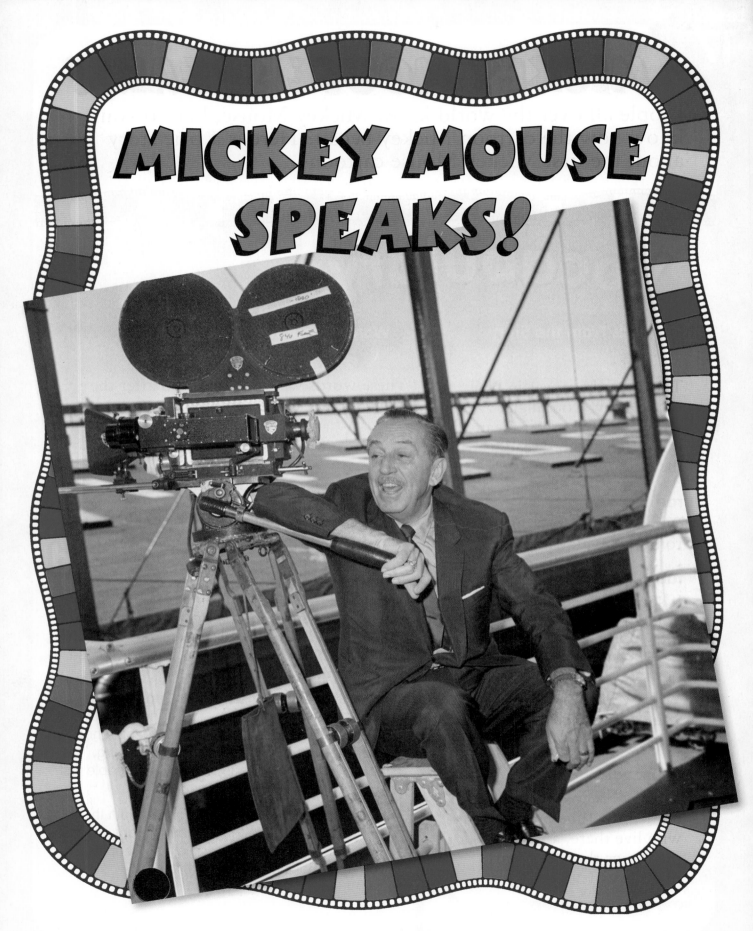

Written by Henry Billings and Melissa Stone Billings

WORLD'S FIRST TALKING CARTOON

Bringing the Story to Life

Use your voice to sound like a radio announcer as you read the opening newspaper article. Read the rest of the selection in a conversational tone, pausing to give emphasis to the title of each new section.

November 18, 1928—Everybody is talking about *Steamboat Willie!* People saw this Walt Disney cartoon today for the first time. Many were laughing as they left New York City's Colony Theater. "It knocked me out of my seat!" cried one reporter. "Bright! Snappy! A good deal of fun!" said another. What makes *Steamboat Willie* so special? It's the world's first cartoon ever made with sound.

An Idea Takes Shape

In the early 1920s, all films were silent. People also watched silent cartoons. Walt Disney had made two silent cartoon series. But like many people, he thought the characters in cartoons were not very interesting. "I need to think of a better character," Disney thought.

In 1928 the 26-year-old Disney was riding a train. Suddenly an idea came to him. "I could see a merry little figure," Disney said. The idea was vague at first. But the idea grew and developed. Finally Disney had his character—a mouse. He would draw a **romping** little mouse.

Disney drew his mouse with big round ears and enormous shoes. At first, Disney wanted to call the mouse Mortimer. But Disney's wife, Lilly, thought the name was too long. "How about Mickey?" she said. "It's short and friendly." So the character became Mickey Mouse.

Who gave Mickey Mouse his name?

Talking Movies

To start, Disney made two silent cartoons about Mickey Mouse. Both turned out well. About that same time, something happened that shook the whole movie business. A movie called *The Jazz Singer* opened in New York City. People rushed to see it. *The Jazz Singer* was the world's first "talking" movie. Some people thought talking movies were just a **fad**.

Why was the movie *The Jazz Singer* important?

Walt Disney knew better. He was sure that movies with sound were here to stay. So Disney went to work on a talking Mickey Mouse cartoon.

Mickey Speaks!

The cartoon was *Steamboat Willie*. It was drawn and put together as a silent cartoon. Then music and voices were added. Disney worked hard to match the sound to the actions in the cartoon. Finally, he got the sound just right. In the fall of 1928, the cartoon was finished.

In the cartoon, Mickey Mouse makes sounds in a funny, high-pitched voice. The voice belonged to Walt Disney. When he talked about his cartoons, Disney would sometimes pretend to be Mickey. The high, squeaky voice he used always made people laugh. Disney hoped his squeaky sounds would now help to make *Steamboat Willie* a success.

Whose voice did Mickey Mouse have?

Disney took his new cartoon to big movie companies. They liked it, but no one would buy the cartoon. Finally the manager of New York's Colony Theater agreed to show it for two weeks. "Those big companies don't know what they want," the manager told Disney. "They need to hear how great it is from movie fans."

The manager was right. Huge crowds **gathered** to see *Steamboat Willie.* In only two weeks, the big movie companies changed their minds. Over time Mickey Mouse became a **household** word. In fact, in 1998, Mickey Mouse celebrated 70 years as a cartoon star. Disney was right. Sound was here to stay.

Talking About the Story

- Ask children to explain how Walt Disney got the idea for the first talking cartoon and how he created the first talking cartoon character.

- Ask children to tell about their favorite cartoon characters. Ask them which is most important for a cartoon character, the way it looks, the way it talks, or the way it laughs.

Vocabulary in Action

romp

In this story Walt Disney decided to draw a romping little mouse. When children or animals romp, they play happily. Let's say *romp* together.

- Ask children which place is best for romping, a park full of jungle gyms or a store full of breakable glass lamps. Explain.
- Invite two children to pretend that they are romping through a field together.

gather

Many people gathered to see Walt Disney's talking cartoon, *Steamboat Willie*. When you gather things, you collect them all into a group. Let's say *gather* together.

- Ask children if people are gathered when they are all sitting around a table or when they are running away from each other. Explain your choice.
- Spread several crayons across a desk and call on a child to gather them together.

fad

Some people believed that talking movies would be just a fad. If something is a fad, it is popular for a very short time. Let's say *fad* together.

- Ask which might be a fad, sleeping at night or collecting toy robots. Why?
- Ask children to name some types of fads.

household

Over time Mickey Mouse became a household word. This means the name was commonly used in people's homes. Your household is your home, all of the people who live there, and all of the things that are a part of it. Let's say *household* together.

- Ask which is part of your household, your bedroom or your desk at school. Why is that?
- Invite children to tell about some people and things that are part of their household.

Words About the Story

entertain

Mickey Mouse brought fun and excitement to many people. Another way to say that is that Mickey Mouse entertained many people. To entertain means to do something like sing, dance, or play an instrument to please an audience. Let's say *entertain* together.

- Ask children which is entertaining, sitting in a chair and looking at a wall or watching clowns play trumpets. Explain your answer.
- Ask a few children to entertain the class by singing a song or dancing.

creative

Walt Disney had many new ideas and made many cartoons. This means Walt Disney was creative. A creative person is someone who is always thinking up new and interesting ideas. Let's say *creative* together.

- Ask children which is creative, painting a new painting or copying a painting someone else already made. Why?
- Have children tell about something they have done or seen that was creative.

Kiss the Cow!

In this fantasy story, Mama May's cow, Luella, stops giving milk when young Annalisa milks Luella and then refuses to kiss the cow as required.

Vocabulary

Words From the Story

These words appear in blue in the story. You might wish to go over their meanings briefly before reading the story.

pasture
A pasture is a field of grass or other plants that animals such as cows and horses like to eat.

velvet
Velvet is a kind of soft, fuzzy cloth.

scrap
A scrap is a little piece of something that is left over when you are finished making something.

Words About the Story

These words will be introduced after the story is read, using context from the story.

mandatory   **tempting**   **provide**

Getting Ready for the Read-Aloud

Show children the picture on page 102 of Mama May kissing the cow. Read the title aloud, and ask children whether they would ever kiss a cow.

Explain that in real life cows give milk that people can drink. In this make-believe story, a cow gives wonderful milk, but only if people follow certain rules.

The following words occur in the story. You can explain them briefly as you come to them: *prairie*, flat, grassy land with few trees; *curious*, eager to learn or find out; *stubborn*, not giving in easily to other people's wishes.

Kiss the Cow!

By Phyllis Root

Illustrated by Will Hillenbrand

Mama May lived where the earth met the sky, and her house was as wide as the prairie. It needed to be. Mama May had so many children she couldn't count them all. Among Mama May's children was one called Annalisa. She wasn't the youngest, and she wasn't the oldest, but she was the most curious and the most stubborn.

Every day Annalisa followed Mama May as she carried her two shiny pails to the **pasture** where she kept Luella, her magic cow with the beautiful brown eyes and bright curving horns. Every day Annalisa heard Mama May sing to Luella.

Lovely Luella,
Your milk never fails.
My children are hungry,
So please fill my pails.

Every day Annalisa saw Luella's warm, sweet milk flow into the shiny pails until Mama May sang:

Thank you, Luella,
My children shall eat
Cheese fresh and yellow
Milk warm and sweet.

Does Luella like Mama May's song? How can you tell?

And every day Annalisa saw Mama May kiss Luella right on the end of her **velvety**, brown nose.

"Ughhh!" said Annalisa. "Imagine kissing a cow!"

Every day Mama May carried her pails of milk home to feed her hungry children. One pail of milk they drank for breakfast. The other pail of milk Mama May heated and salted and pressed into cheese for the children's supper, cheese so fresh it squeaked between their teeth.

Every day Annalisa wondered, *What would it be like to milk a magic cow?* The more she wondered, the more curious she grew. And the more curious she grew, the more Annalisa just had to know.

Finally one day she said, "I want to milk Luella."

"Never you mind about milking Luella," said Mama May. "If you upset her, she'll never give milk, and then what would we do?"

But Annalisa had made up her mind. She took a pail from the sandbox and sneaked off alone to the pasture.

Just like Mama May, Annalisa sang,

Lovely Luella,
Your milk never fails.
My children are hungry,
So please fill my pails.

Luella's milk flowed into Annalisa's little pail until she sang,

Thank you, Luella,
My children shall eat
Cheese fresh and yellow
Milk warm and sweet.

But did Annalisa kiss Luella right on the end of her soft, silky nose? She did not.

And the next day Luella would not give any milk at all, no matter how many times Mama May sang her magic song. It didn't take Mama May long to figure out what had happened.

"Annalisa!" she cried. "Have you been bothering Luella?"

> How did Mama May guess what had happened to Luella?

"All I did was milk her with my little pail," said Annalisa.

"And did you remember to kiss the cow?" asked Mama May.

"Me? Kiss a slobbery, bristly cow?" cried Annalisa.

"You must kiss the cow to make sure she gives milk again," said Mama May.

"**Never!**" cried Annalisa. And she wouldn't.

That day the children ate **scraps** of bread without milk for breakfast. "Now will you kiss the cow?" asked Mama May.

"**Never!**" said Annalisa.

No kiss, no milk.

That night the children ate crusts of bread without cheese for supper. "Now will you kiss the cow?" asked Mama May.

"**Never!**" said Annalisa.

No kiss, no milk, no cheese. The next day Mama May's house was full of hungry, crying children.

The hungry children crowded around Annalisa. There were so many children they crowded her right out of the house and up the hill to the pasture. "**Milk!**" they begged. "**Cheese!**" they pleaded.

"Now will you kiss the cow?" asked Mama May.

"**Never!**" cried Annalisa. "**Never, never, never.**"

"**Mooooooooooooo,**" said Luella, putting her nose in Annalisa's face.

"**Ugh!**" said Annalisa.

But then she looked into Luella's beautiful brown eyes and wondered, *What would it be like to kiss a cow?* The more she wondered, the more curious she grew. And the more curious she grew, the more Annalisa just had to know. There was only one way to find out.

What happened before when Annalisa was curious about milking the cow?

"Please kiss the cow," said Mama May.

"Hmmmm," said Annalisa.

But she scrunched up her eyes, bunched up her face, and kissed Luella. Luella smelled of fresh hay and sunshine and clover. Her nose felt silky and warm and dry.

Mama May sang her magic song. Luella's milk began to flow. The children cheered. And Annalisa felt so fine…**she kissed the cow again.**

Talking About the Story

- Ask children to tell about how Annalisa caused trouble with Mama May's cow, Luella, and how she finally made things right again.
- Have children tell about something that they did at one time, even though they didn't want to. Did it turn out to be as bad as they had expected?

Vocabulary in Action

pasture

In the story Luella stayed in a pasture. A pasture is a field of grass or other plants that animals such as cows and horses like to eat. Let's say *pasture* together.

- Ask children which you might see in the middle of a pasture, flowers or a school bus. Why is that?
- Call on a child to pretend to be a cow eating grass in a pasture.

scrap

Mama May's children had to eat scraps of bread after Luella stopped giving milk. A scrap is a little piece of something that is left over when you are finished making something. Let's say *scrap* together.

- Ask children which is a scrap, a pile of clay to make into a pot or a piece of clay that is left over after you have made a clay horse. Tell why.
- Have children fold a sheet of paper into fourths, cut out some pieces, and unfold the paper to show the design. Then have children show you the scraps.

velvet

Luella the cow had a velvety, brown nose. Velvet is a kind of soft, fuzzy cloth. Let's say *velvet* together.

- Ask which of these things might be made from velvet: a sidewalk, a dress, or a hat. Explain your answer.
- Bring in a small piece of velvet for children to touch.

Words About the Story

mandatory

Luella would not give milk unless Mama May sang and kissed her. In other words, it was mandatory that Mama May sing and kiss Luella in order to get milk. If something is mandatory, you have to do it. Let's say *mandatory* together.

- Ask children which is mandatory, stopping at a red light or eating ice cream every day. Explain.
- Have children describe some things that are mandatory at school.

tempting

Annalisa was so curious about milking the cow that she just had to do it. In other words, the cow was tempting to Annalisa. If something is tempting, you want it very much, even if you know you should not have it. Let's say *tempting* together.

- Ask which is tempting to eat, a jar of cookies or a pile of rotten eggs. Why?
- Ask children to tell some things that would be tempting to do on a really, really hot day.

provide

Luella the cow gave Mama May's family plenty of wonderful milk. Another way to say that is that Luella provided milk for the family. To provide something, you give it to someone so they can use it. Let's say *provide* together.

- Ask children who is providing something, a girl who brings sandwiches to a picnic or a girl who steals sandwiches from a picnic. Explain your choice.
- Invite children to talk about some things that their parents or teachers provide for them.

Coyote and the Stars

This Native American legend tells how the desert, including its nighttime sky, was decorated by the animals that live there.

Vocabulary

Words From the Story

These words appear in blue in the story. You might wish to go over their meanings briefly before reading the story.

delicate
Something that is delicate is small and light and easily broken.

vast
If something is vast, it is so large that is seems like it has no end.

investigate
When you investigate something, you try to find out what it is all about.

variety
A variety is many different kinds of something.

Words About the Story

These words will be introduced after the story is read, using context from the story.

enhance   **accomplish**

Getting Ready for the Read-Aloud

Show children the picture on page 109. Read the title aloud, and tell children that this story is a legend, an old story that has been told over and over. Legends are usually not true, but they often teach a lesson or explain something.

Use books or magazines to show illustrations of deserts. Point out ravens, prairie dogs, burros, bobcats, cacti, valleys, mesas (flat, elevated landforms with steep sides), and canyons. Help children brainstorm words about desert animals, vegetation, landforms, and climate.

The following words occur in the story. They can be briefly explained as you come to them in the story: *critical*, not thinking something is very good; *resources*, supplies; *illuminating*, giving light; *smothered*, covered up completely; *textures*, the way things feel when you touch them.

Coyote and the Stars

A Native American legend retold by Rochelle Rupp
Illustrated by Annette Cable

Many, many years ago the desert creatures worked together to help arrange the beauty of their home. All the creatures helped except lazy Coyote. He would lay around all day and night and watch the others work hard in the scorching desert sun.

He slept peacefully while the hawks and ravens placed the cool and winding rivers within the deep valleys.

Coyote reclined in the cool shade as the bighorn sheep and mountain lions struggled to move the magnificent mountains.

Bringing the Story to Life

Tape up a large piece of white paper. As you tell the story, add simple, colorful illustrations to match the animals' actions so children can better visualize the progress as the animals "create" the desert scenery. Use glitter to make the stars.

What are the hawks, ravens, bighorn sheep, and mountain lions doing? What is the coyote doing?

While the jack rabbits, gophers, and deer were planting protective forests, Coyote watched with a critical eye.

Prairie dogs, burros, and bobcats spread **delicate** sand and prickly cacti to make the desert floor a beautiful place to live. Still, the Coyote just watched in boredom.

Finally, Coyote yawned disrespectfully and complained, "Is this the best you can do?"

So the spiders, ants, and snakes brushed the sands and rocks with the colors of a glorious sunset—vibrant coral, delicate peach, quiet pink, deep orange, and hints of violet. They made enormous canyons and **vast** mesas too great to explore. They continued to paint and improve for days and days using all their resources, leaving their most illuminating creation for the end—thousands and thousands of dazzling chips of light. Each was polished like silver and glittered like gold. The creatures were eager to include the new lights in their designs.

The ravens and hawks dipped the chips into the cool streams and flowing rivers, but the waters lapped up the light, and Coyote woke with interest.

The deer, jackrabbits, and gophers hung the chips on branches in the protective forests, but the shade smothered the light, and Coyote raised his head in attention.

> Why do you think Coyote started to be interested in what the other animals were doing?

Mountain lions and bighorn sheep carefully placed the chips high on the mountain peaks, but the bright sun stole the light, and Coyote stood with concentration.

Bobcats, prairie dogs, and burros sprinkled the chips across the desert floor, but the colored sands covered the light, and Coyote looked on with curiosity.

The creatures had worked hard that day, and since they could not find the proper place for their dazzling chips, they all went home to rest. When the last eye shut and the desert was quiet, Coyote came to **investigate** the brilliant lights. "What ARE these useless things?"

> Why do you think Coyote waited until all of the other animals went to sleep?

"They cannot swim in water," he said as he tossed a few behind his back.

"They cannot hang in trees," he said as he tossed some behind his back.

"They cannot top the mountain peaks," he said as he tossed more behind his back.

"They cannot flow with the desert sands," he said as he tossed even more behind his back.

Finding that they could not be eaten or enjoyed in any useful way, he threw the rest over his shoulder until they were all gone.

The foolish Coyote continued to walk along the lovely desert not appreciating the **varieties** of colors and textures designed by all the other creatures. Nor did he realize that behind him, the dazzling chips of light had landed beautifully in the nighttime sky.

And that is how Coyote placed the stars in the sky.

Talking About the Story

- Ask children to name animals from the story. For each animal they name, ask children to describe what job that animal did to make the desert beautiful.
- Ask children which animal's job they would most like to have had. Why?

Vocabulary in Action

Words From the Story

delicate

In the story the animals spread delicate sand on the desert floor. Something that is delicate is small and light and easily broken. Let's say *delicate* together.

- Ask children which is more delicate, a rock or an eggshell. Why?
- Ask children to show you how they would hold something that is delicate.

investigate

Coyote investigated the bright chips of light. When you investigate something, you try to find out what it is all about. Let's say *investigate* together.

- Ask who would need to investigate, a person who knows everything or a person who needs to find information about something. Explain.
- Fill a box with assorted items, such as pencils, a stapler, a sock, and several coins. Place the box on your desk. Ask a volunteer to show how they would investigate the things in the box.

vast

The animals made vast mesas. If something is vast, it is so large that it seems like it has no end. Let's say *vast* together.

- Ask children which is vast, outer space or their classroom. Explain your choice.
- Ask children to look through magazines to find images of things that are vast.

variety

In the story the animals add a variety of colors and textures to the desert. A variety is many different kinds of something. Let's say *variety* together.

- Ask which has more variety, a store that sells only small, red hats, or a store that sells hats in many colors and sizes. Why?
- Ask a volunteer to show you a variety of facial expressions. Ask another volunteer to silently walk around the room and point out a variety of books.

Words About the Story

enhance

In the story the animals make the desert more beautiful by adding things to it. Another way to say that is the animals enhanced the desert. When you enhance something, you make it better. Let's say *enhance* together.

- Ask which is enhanced, a plain white sock or a sock that has been made into a puppet with buttons for eyes and yarn for hair. Tell why.
- Draw a simple smiley face on the board with two eyes and a mouth. Have a child draw more features to enhance the face.

accomplish

In the story the other animals can't do anything with the bright chips of light, but Coyote accidentally finds a perfect place for them. Coyote accomplishes something the other animals couldn't do. When you accomplish something, you complete something that was very hard to do. Let's say *accomplish* together.

- Ask children which person accomplished something, someone who gave up after one try or someone who kept trying until she finished. Why?
- Ask children to name some things they have accomplished.

STRONG ENOUGH

In this story an alligator learns not to brag about being the strongest alligator in the swamp.

Vocabulary

Words From the Story

These words appear in blue in the story. You might wish to go over their meanings briefly before reading the story.

boast
When you boast about something, you talk about it in a way that is so proud that it is like showing off.

mighty
When something is mighty, it is very large and strong.

flatter
When you flatter someone, you tell them nice things about themselves to make them feel good.

frighten
To frighten someone is to scare them very badly.

Words About the Story

These words will be introduced after the story is read, using context from the story.

enormous   **humble**

Getting Ready for the Read-Aloud

Show children the picture on page 115. Read the title aloud, and tell children that this is a story about an alligator who likes to brag about being the strongest alligator in the swamp. Ask children to describe what this alligator is doing in the picture to show off. Then have volunteers describe how the other alligators in the picture feel about this alligator showing off.

Explain that in many stories there is a problem that needs to be solved. Tell children that in this story, the problem is that this alligator brags too much. Ask children how this problem might be solved.

You might wish to explain the following words as you come to them in the story: *bayou*, a muddy stream leading out of a swamp; *slink*, to slip or sneak away; *a run for my money*, made it difficult for me to win.

STRONG ENOUGH

By Teresa Turner

Illustrated by Joseph Hammond

Once upon a time in a stinky, sticky swamp lived an alligator named Zeke. Zeke drove all the other alligators crazy. He was always **boasting** about all the great things he could do. One day Alicia the alligator was having dinner with her family under a big, mossy tree. Zeke walked right up and sat down. "Did you know that I'm the **mightiest** alligator in the swamp?"

"Yes, Zeke, we know," said Alicia.

"You do?" asked Zeke. "Oh." He looked disappointed. "Don't you want me to prove it?"

"There's no need for that, Zeke," Alicia answered.

Zeke walked away. Far off in the water, he could see the very tip of someone's nose. It was Hayward, the oldest alligator in the swamp. Zeke slipped into the bayou. "Hey, Hayward!" Zeke yelled.

"What? Who? Oh, you," said Hayward. "Why did you wake me up from my nap?"

"I wanted to tell you that I'm the mightiest alligator in the swamp," said Zeke.

Hayward yawned. "I don't know about that," he said. "I've seen plenty of strong alligators in my time."

"Oh, yeah?" said Zeke. "See that big old tree over there? I can pull that tree up roots and all. Do you want to see?"

"I can't wait," said Hayward.

Bringing the Story to Life

Loudly act out the noises of the tree roots ripping out of the ground, Hayward sleeping, Zelda's heavy footsteps, and Zelda falling to the ground. Read Hayward's dialogue in a sleepy, sarcastic way.

Why do you think Alicia doesn't want to see Zeke prove that he is the mightiest?

Do you think Hayward really wants to see Zeke pull up the tree?

Zeke swam over and wrapped his huge tail around the tree's trunk. He pulled as hard as he could. UUUGH, UUUGH, RIP! The tree's roots came out of the ground. The tree landed in the water with a giant SPLASH. Zeke swam back to Hayward. "Did you see?" he asked. "I did it!"

ZZZZZZ. Hayward had gone back to sleep.

Next Zeke found two brothers, Jeff and Jason. They were sunning themselves on the bank. "Hello, boys," said Zeke. "Did you know that I'm the mightiest alligator in the swamp?"

"You asked us that last week," said Jeff.

"Shhhh," whispered Jason. "Let's have some fun." Then he said to Zeke, "You don't look very mighty to me. Let's see what you can do."

Zeke looked around. "You see that big old granddaddy tortoise over there? I can lift him over my head."

"Go on," said Jeff. "We're watching."

Zeke walked over to the tortoise. It was as big as a car tire. "Excuse me, granddaddy tortoise," said Zeke. "Would you mind being very still for a moment?" Zeke grabbed the edges of the tortoise's shell and lifted him overhead. It looked as though Zeke were wearing a big, green hat.

Jeff and Jason laughed. "You're mighty, all right— mighty silly!" Jeff said.

Zeke blushed and set the tortoise back down.

Next Zeke found a bunch of young alligators playing hide-and-seek. "I'm the mightiest alligator in the swamp!" said Zeke.

Were we right about whether Hayward really wanted to see the tree pulled up?

Why did Jeff and Jason really want Zeke to lift up the tortoise?

"You're the mightiest alligator in the world!" said one young alligator.

"You're stronger than a horse!" said another.

"Don't **flatter** him!" said Max, the smallest alligator. "His head is big enough as it is."

"So you don't think I'm the mightiest, little alligator?" Zeke asked. "Maybe you'd like to wrestle me."

"Not me, I'm too small," said Max, "but my sister Zelda will. She's not **frightened** of you. Hey, Zelda!" Max called.

> Do you think Zeke will want to wrestle Zelda?

BOOM, BOOM, BOOM, BOOM. The ground shook. Into a clearing came a really huge alligator. She looked like a tree trunk with legs! "You called, little brother?"

"Zeke thinks he's the mightiest alligator in the swamp. He wants to wrestle you to prove it," said Max.

"Sure, I love to wrestle," said Zelda.

All the alligators gathered around to watch. Zeke looked at Zelda. She was almost twice as big as he was. The strong muscles in her tail rippled as she swished it back and forth. Zeke tried to swallow, but his mouth was dry. His legs felt wobbly. Still, he had to wrestle her. If he didn't, everyone would know that he wasn't the mightiest alligator in the swamp.

"Ready, set, go!" said Max. Zeke and Zelda circled each other. Zeke wrapped his tail around Zelda's neck. Zelda shook her head so hard he went flying off. "Hooray, Zelda!" cheered the crowd. Then Zeke grabbed Zelda's back legs. CRASH! Zelda fell to the ground.

"Way to go, Zeke!" someone yelled. Quick as a flash, Zeke climbed up on her back.

"Now I have you!" he said.

"Not so fast," said Zelda. She threw Zeke off her back, grabbed his tail, and turned him on his back. "Zelda! Zelda!" the crowd chanted. Zeke tried to roll over, but Zelda held him down with her powerful front legs.

Zeke tried and tried to get up, but Zelda was too strong. "Do you give up?" Zelda asked.

"Y-y-yes, I give up," Zeke said sadly.

Why is Zeke sad?

The alligators all cheered. "Hooray, Zelda! Zelda's the mightiest!" Even Hayward said, "She's the strongest alligator I've ever seen."

Zeke felt awful. He started to slink away. "Hey, Zeke!" Zelda yelled. "I want to shake your hand. You really gave me a run for my money."

Why does Zelda want to shake Zeke's hand?

"But I lost," Zeke said bitterly. "I'm not the mightiest anymore."

"I'll tell you what," said Zelda. "From now on, let's not boast about being the mightiest. Let's just say we're both *strong enough*."

So just like that, Zeke learned to stop boasting, and the stinky, sticky swamp was a much happier place.

Talking About the Story

- Ask children to describe how Zeke acts while he thinks he is the mightiest. How is this different from the way Zelda acts?

- Ask children how they would act if they were as mighty as Zeke.

Vocabulary in Action

boast

In the story Zeke boasted a lot about being mighty. When you boast about something, you talk about it in a way that is so proud it is like showing off. Let's say *boast* together.

- Ask children who might boast, someone who just won a race or someone who came in last place. Why?
- Have children use exaggerated facial expressions and gestures to boast about how great their shoes are.

mighty

In the story Zeke was a mighty alligator. When something is mighty, it is very large and strong. Let's say *mighty* together.

- Ask children which is more mighty, a giant dinosaur or a tiny lizard. Explain your choice.
- Have children talk about mighty people or animals they know.

flatter

The young alligators flatter Zeke by agreeing that he is mighty and strong. When you flatter someone, you tell them nice things about themselves to make them feel good. Let's say *flatter* together.

- Ask which is more flattering, to tell someone that they are good at painting or to tell someone that their drawing is messy. Explain your answer.
- Ask children what they would say to flatter someone wearing a nice hat.

frighten

Zelda was not frightened by Zeke. To frighten someone is to scare them very badly. Let's say *frighten* together.

- Ask which situation might frighten you, seeing a snake in a zoo or seeing a snake in your bathtub. Why?
- Invite children to make faces that might frighten someone.

Words About the Story

enormous

Zeke is huge, but Zelda is twice as big as he is. Another way to say that is to say that Zelda is enormous. If something is enormous, it is almost larger than you can imagine. Let's say *enormous* together.

- Ask which is enormous, a pebble or a mountain. Explain.
- Have a child act out stepping over an enormous puddle.

humble

In the story Zelda did not brag or show off about being mighty. Another way to say that is to say that she was humble. If someone is humble, they do not look for a lot of attention. Let's say *humble* together.

- Ask who is humble, someone who says you don't have to thank them or someone who says they can do everything without your help. Why?
- Ask children if they know anyone who is humble, someone who is good at something but doesn't act like they are better than everyone else.

The Tortoise and the Baboon

In this African folk tale, when Baboon plays a trick on Tortoise, Tortoise pays Baboon back by teaching him a lesson.

Vocabulary

Words From the Story

These words appear in blue in the story. You might wish to go over their meanings briefly before reading the story.

determined
If you are determined to do something, you have decided to do it and nothing will stop you.

savory
Savory food tastes good because it is salty or spicy, not sweet.

scamper
When people or animals scamper, they move quickly with small, light steps.

frantic
If someone is frantic, they are behaving in a wild way because they are scared, worried, or in a hurry.

Words About the Story

These words will be introduced after the story is read, using context from the story.

stunned   **shrewd**

Getting Ready for the Read-Aloud

Show children the picture on page 122 of the tortoise and the baboon and help them identify the characters. Read the title aloud, and ask children to tell whether they think that this story will be about real animals or make-believe ones.

Explain to children that sometimes tales have been told over and over again for hundreds of years. Point out that this tale comes from Africa. You may want to locate Africa on a map or globe for children. Explain that sometimes tales such as these teach a lesson about how to behave.

The following words can be briefly explained as you come to them in the story: *barren*, empty; *devised*; came up with; *soot*, dust and dirt; *succulent*, juicy; *charred*, burned.

The Tortoise and the Baboon

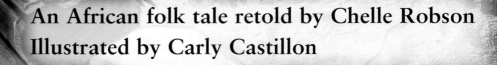

An African folk tale retold by Chelle Robson
Illustrated by Carly Castillon

Bringing the Story to Life

Add animation to the dialogue by using different voices for Tortoise and Baboon. Adjust the pace as well, speaking slowly and deliberately for Tortoise and using a quick and lively pace for Baboon.

It was the dry season in the African grasslands, and many bush fires had left the ground barren and black. It was often very difficult to find enough food in the dry season, and Tortoise was quite hungry. One quiet evening the gentle Tortoise was crawling slowly home when he met Baboon on his path.

"Hello, old fellow," said Baboon warmly. "Have you found much to eat today?"

"I'm afraid not," replied Tortoise. "Sadly, I've found very little to eat."

Baboon chortled to himself as he began to scheme. "Follow me, poor old Tortoise," he invited. "I will go ahead, and when you reach my home I will have a generous meal waiting for you."

"Why, thank you very much, my bouncy friend," said Tortoise as he watched Baboon bound and leap along the path. Slowly and carefully, hungry Tortoise plodded on until he finally reached the caves and trees where Baboon lived.

When Tortoise finally arrived, Baboon was impatiently leaping from tree to rock, and from rock to tree, and he began to call out loudly when he saw Tortoise, "So slow, so slow, so slow you are! You are certainly the slowest creature in the grasslands!"

"Indeed, Baboon," said Tortoise. "I may be old and slow, but I am **determined** to enjoy your fine meal."

"Then please hurry and come up to join me," teased Baboon from high in a tree. "The feast is waiting."

Will Tortoise be able to join Baboon in the tree? Why or why not?

Hungry Tortoise looked up and saw **savory** leaves and luscious fruits wedged high in the branches.

"How can I climb up to you, Baboon? You know I cannot reach your meal." Tortoise pleaded, "Throw some fruit down to me, you tricky friend."

"I may be tricky, but you, Tortoise, are foolish. Don't you know? If you want to eat with baboons, you must climb trees."

Poor Tortoise, with an empty stomach and a heavy shell, he turned around to begin the long journey home. As he walked along the path, he devised a clever plan of his own.

Several days later Baboon received an invitation to eat lunch with Tortoise. Naturally, he was very surprised, but knowing how gracious Tortoise was, Baboon decided to accept the invitation and he began his journey. First, he enjoyed swinging through the trees. Then, he walked carefully across the shallow part of the river. Finally, he began to bound and leap across the scorched and blackened grasslands all the way to the home of Tortoise.

Why was Baboon surprised by Tortoise's invitation?

"Ah, Baboon. How good of you to join me," Tortoise greeted. "I hope you are ready for a feast of fresh fish and clams. However, I see that you are not ready to eat; your hands are black with soot from your journey. You cannot eat a fine meal like this with dirty hands."

Baboon silently looked down at his hands and was embarrassed to see how blackened they had become while walking across the scorched grasslands.

"Now go to the river and wash them properly, and then I will be happy to share my meal with you," said Tortoise. "Go quickly, though, because I am going to begin eating now."

Do you think Tortoise really wants to share his meal with Baboon?

Baboon **scampered** across the blackened earth and washed his hands in the river. He returned quickly, thinking about the succulent clams Tortoise had prepared.

When Baboon arrived, Tortoise scolded him again, "Your hands are still dirty. Did you wash them at all? They are just as black as they were before."

Surprised, Baboon looked down at his hands to discover that they had become dirty again on his return from the river.

Why are Baboon's hands dirty again?

"Baboon, you know you cannot eat with me until your hands are clean, so go back and wash again. I'll just finish these juicy clams," Tortoise said with a faint smile. "I will *try* to save you some fish, but you should hurry."

Frantically, hungry Baboon crossed the charred grasslands to wash his hands in the river. When they were clean, he tried to make his return without soiling his hands, but it was impossible. He called from the river, "Tortoise, I see the trick you are playing on me, and I have learned my lesson. You know that I cannot join you with clean hands. *Please* save some fish for me."

"Foolish, Baboon. You are too late," called the Tortoise as he swallowed the last fish. I have enjoyed watching you scamper frantically across the blackened grasslands almost as much as I have enjoyed my lunch of clams and fish."

Knowing that he was being punished for his devious prank in the tree, Baboon hungrily ran all the way home, calling and shouting in frustration.

Talking About the Story

- Have children retell how Baboon tricked Tortoise and how Tortoise tricked Baboon.
- Ask children whether they think what Baboon and Tortoise did to each other was fair or unfair.

Vocabulary in Action

determined

In the story Tortoise said that he is determined to enjoy Baboon's fine meal. If you are determined to do something, you have decided to do it and nothing will stop you. Let's say *determined* together.

- Ask which person is determined, someone who practices every day to learn how to dance or someone who says dancing is too hard and gives up. Why?
- Ask a child to use their face to show how they might look if they were determined to carry a big stack of books across the room.

scamper

Baboon scampered across the grassland to wash his hands in the river. When people or animals scamper, they move quickly with small, light steps. Let's say *scamper* together.

- Ask which animal could scamper, a mouse or a snake. Explain.
- Demonstrate scampering and have children scamper around the room. For contrast, have them walk with slow, heavy steps as well.

savory

Tortoise wanted to eat the savory leaves high in the trees. Savory food tastes good because it is salty or spicy, not sweet. Let's say *savory* together.

- Ask children which is savory, mashed potatoes or apple pie. Why is that?
- Have children name some of their favorite savory foods.

frantic

Baboon grew frantic as he tried to get his hands clean. If someone is frantic, they are behaving in a wild way because they are scared, worried, or in a hurry. Let's say *frantic* together.

- Ask children which is an example of frantic behavior, stacking cans carefully in a row on a shelf or throwing cans quickly onto the shelf until they all fall down. Explain your answer.
- Have children pantomime getting dressed in a frantic way because they are late for school.

Words About the Story

stunned

Baboon was very surprised that his hands kept getting dirty. Another way to say that is that Baboon was stunned. If you are stunned by something, you are so shocked or surprised by it that you can hardly speak or move. Let's say *stunned* together.

- Ask children which would stun them, seeing a bus go down the street or seeing a huge dinosaur run down the street. Why is that?
- Have a child act out what Baboon's stunned face might have looked like when he saw that his paws were dirty once again.

shrewd

Tortoise thought of a clever plan to teach Baboon a lesson. Another way to say this is that Tortoise thought of a shrewd plan. Shrewd people are able to use all that they know to make things turn out well for themselves. Let's say *shrewd* together.

- Ask who is shrewd, a person who gets left behind and has to walk home or a person who always gets other people to drive them around. Why is that?
- Have a child act out what Tortoise's thoughts might have been as he came up with his shrewd plan.

Seal Surfer

In this story a boy learns about life by watching a seal pup change and grow through the seasons.

Vocabulary

Words From the Story

These words appear in blue in the story. You might wish to go over their meanings briefly before reading the story.

injured
A person or animal that is injured has hurt some part of its body.

bask
To bask in the sunshine is to lie back and enjoy how warm it feels.

haul
When you haul something, you move something heavy by pulling it.

elated
To be elated is to feel completely happy about something.

Words About the Story

These words will be introduced after the story is read, using context from the story.

seasonal   **contemplate**

Getting Ready for the Read-Aloud

Show children the picture on pages 128 and 129. Read the title aloud, and ask children to think about how the boy who is surfing might feel to be in the water with the seal.

Since this story touches on the themes of birth and death, you may want to discuss the fact that animals and people have life cycles in which they are born, change and grow, and then die.

The following words occur in the story. They can be briefly explained as you come to them in the story: *molted*, shed; *corkscrewing*, turning around in a spiral pattern; *Beethoven*, a famous person of long ago who wrote a style of music mostly for instruments only; *ventured*, went out.

Seal Surfer

Written and illustrated by Michael Foreman

Bringing the Story to Life

To help children understand the passage of time in the story, put special emphasis on the season titles. Use your voice to animate the occasional character dialogue to contrast it from the narrative parts of the story.

SPRING

One day in early spring an old man and his grandson, Ben, carefully climbed down to a rocky beach. They were looking for mussels.

As Ben searched he noticed a slight movement among the rocks. Then he saw the seal. It was difficult to see her body against the rocks, except for a smudge of red on her belly.

"Look, Granddad!" Ben cried. "The seal is injured."

What do you think is wrong with the seal?

"Don't get too close," warned Granddad. They watched the seal from a distance.

The seal looked quite calm, lying still in the morning sun, and after a while Ben started hunting for mussels again.

When he next looked up at the seal, he saw a flash of white. A newly born seal pup nuzzled her mother.

"Quick, Granddad," whispered Ben. "Let's get some fish for the seals."

As the spring days lengthened, Ben and his granddad often watched the seal family from the cliff top. The pup's white coat molted and she became the color of the rocks. Sometimes she moved to the water's edge to watch her mother fish. As she **basked** in the warm sun, she kept an eye on Ben and his granddad.

SUMMER

In early summer Ben watched as the mother seal pushed her pup off the rocks and into the sea. The shock of the cold water made the young seal panic. The water closed over her head. She pushed upward with her tail and flippers until her head burst through the surface.

Her mother plunged into the water, and together they swam around and around—diving, twisting, corkscrewing into the depths. When the seal pup broke through the water's surface, she heard the boy cheer.

AUTUMN

The summer days faded. One evening Ben went down to the harbor to meet his granddad, who was returning from a day's fishing. Granddad's old pickup truck sat with the door open and the radio on. The music of Beethoven filled the air.

Granddad stared into the water. A whiskery face stared back at him like a reflection in the moonlit mirror of the harbor.

Granddad tossed the seal a fish—and then another. Ben watched as the mirror dissolved, reformed, and then dissolved again as they all shared the music of Beethoven.

How do you think Ben and Granddad feel about each other? What clues tell you so?

WINTER

While the wet winter winds buffeted the boy on his way to school, the young seal learned the lessons of the sea.

The seal loved to swim far from home, exploring the coast. She learned to fish by swimming deep and looking up to see the fish outlined against the sky.

She slept at sea, floating upright like a bottle, with just her nose above the surface. Best of all she loved to **haul** herself up onto the rocks with other young seals to feel the sun and wind on her skin.

But one day the wind rose suddenly into a full-blown gale. Rain and mountainous waves wrenched great rocks from the cliffs. The young seals dived deep, trying to escape falling boulders. But even in the sea they were in danger. Some seals were dashed against the rocks by the waves.

Why are the young seals in danger?

SPRING

The warmth of spring brought wildflowers and Ben and his granddad to the cliffs once more. But there was no sign of the young seal.

"She must have died in the winter storms," said Ben.

But sometimes the mother seal still came to the harbor for an evening of fish and music.

SUMMER

As spring warmed into summer, Ben went every Saturday to Surf School. He was a strong swimmer, and after much practice he and the other new surfers were ready to catch some waves.

One sunny day Ben lay on his board as it rose and fell on the gently rocking swell. Suddenly he was aware of a quick movement in the water. A dark shape swooped under the board. The gleaming face of the young seal popped up beside his own. Ben was **elated**. "You're alive!" he called, grinning.

Did this part of the story surprise you? Why or why not?

The sea gathered itself for some big waves. The dark green walls of water lined up along the horizon. The seal sensed the movement of the water. Ben and the seal let the first two waves pass, then together they rode the third huge, rolling wave toward the shore.

All afternoon Ben and the seal surfed together. Then just as quickly as she had appeared, the seal was gone. Ben waited awhile and then let the next good wave carry him to the sand.

The next day the tide was perfect and the young seal was back. Again Ben and the seal surfed side by side.

Ben could not take his eyes off the seal as she flashed through the water. As he concentrated on watching her, the wave he was riding suddenly broke and plunged him headfirst off his board. He somersaulted through the surf and struck a rock. The water, thick with sand, filled his nose and mouth. His body was pulled deeper and deeper. He was sinking into darkness.

Then he felt a different sensation. His body was forced upward. Sunlight shone through the water onto Ben's face as the seal pushed his body up. With a final heave she flipped Ben onto his board. He held on, and the next wave carried him to the shore. His friends crowded around to make sure he was all right. Once he caught his breath, Ben felt fine.

What just happened to Ben?

The next afternoon, and for the rest of the long, hot summer, Ben surfed with the seal.

WINTER

The wonderful summer and gentle autumn were followed by the worst of winters. The storms smacked the rocks and churned up the sand and stones. The beach was deserted. No seals came there.

SPRING

When the next spring brought the wildflowers to the cliffs, it brought Ben but not his grandfather. The boy and his friends ventured far along the cliffs, but they could find no sign of the seals.

SUMMER

As the evenings grew lighter toward the start of the summer, Ben began fishing from the quay, as his grand-dad had done before him. One evening as he watched the still water, two shiny heads broke through the surface. Ben cheered as he saw the once young seal—now as whiskery as Granddad—with *her* young pup.

Ben smiled. He knew, then, that he would ride the waves with the seals that summer and every summer.

And maybe one day he would lie on the cliff tops with his own grandchildren and together they would watch the seals.

Talking About the Story

- Ask children to pretend that many years later, Ben is a grandfather talking to his grandchildren. What would he tell them about his time with the seals?
- Invite children to share experiences they have had in watching someone or something grow and change over time.

Vocabulary in Action

Words From the Story

injured

At the beginning of the story, Ben thought the mother seal was injured. A person or animal that is injured has hurt some part of its body. Let's say *injured* together.

- Ask who is injured, a person dancing or a person with a cast on their leg. Why?
- Ask children to show how they would walk if one of their legs were injured.

haul

The young seal liked to haul herself up from the water onto the rocks. When you haul something, you move something heavy by pulling it. Let's say *haul* together.

- Ask which you might haul, a pair of boots or three children on a sled. Why?
- Have children tell about the heaviest thing they have ever hauled.

bask

The seal pup basked in the sunshine. To bask in the sunshine is to lie back and enjoy how warm it feels. Let's say *bask* together.

- Ask where you might bask, in a sunny field or in a snowy forest. Explain.
- Ask children to pretend to be kittens basking in the sunshine.

elated

In the story Ben was elated when he found out that the young seal was alive. To be elated is to feel completely happy about something. Let's say *elated* together.

- Which would make you feel elated, eating a triple-scoop ice cream cone or dropping your ice cream on the ground? Explain.
- Have children act out being elated to run into a friend they haven't seen in a long time.

Words About the Story

seasonal

In the story certain things happen at certain times of the year. Another way to say this is to say that much of the story is seasonal. If something is seasonal, it happens every year at the same time. Let's say *seasonal* together.

- Which is seasonal, a Thanksgiving celebration or a celebration for getting a good grade on a test? Why?
- Ask children to draw a tree's seasonal changes from growing new branches and blooms in spring, to lush green leaves in summer, to red, orange, and yellow leaves in autumn, to being covered by snow in winter.

contemplate

Ben and his grandfather spent a lot of time thinking about the seals and about the stages of life. Another way to say that is to say that they were contemplating these things. When you contemplate something, you think about it very deeply. Let's say *contemplate* together.

- Ask which of these things is an example of contemplating, thinking about what kind of sandwich to have for lunch or thinking about how to make sure that all people are treated fairly. Explain your answer.
- Ask children to use their faces to show how they look when they contemplate something very important.

Jamaica
and the
Substitute Teacher

In this story a girl learns that all students are special to the substitute teacher.

CDEFGHIJKLMNOPQRSTUVWXYZABCDEFGHIJKLMNOPQRSTUVWXYZABCDEFGHI

Vocabulary

Words From the Story

These words appear in blue in the story. You might wish to go over their meanings briefly before reading the story.

memorize
When you memorize something, you make sure that you know it without having to look back at it.

stare
When you stare, you look straight at something for a long time.

exchange
When you exchange something, you give something to someone and they give you something, too.

Words About the Story

These words will be introduced after the story is read, using context from the story.

relief   **regret**   **anxious**

Getting Ready for the Read-Aloud

Show children the picture of the classroom scene on page 136. Read the title aloud, and ask children to think about how they might behave if they wanted a substitute teacher to like them very much.

Explain that sometimes people want someone else to like them so much that they are afraid to make mistakes or are afraid to be themselves.

You might wish to briefly explain the following words as you come to them in the story: *silky*, soft and smooth; *Ohio*, one of the states in the United States; *Antarctica*, a large piece of land where it is extremely cold.

Jamaica
and the
Substitute Teacher

By Juanita Havill

Illustrated by Anne Sibley O'Brien

Bringing the Story to Life

urry, Brianna," Jamaica said. "I want to see who our substitute is."

Brianna caught up. "I hope she's nice."

"Me, too."

A woman wearing a silky blue and green dress and a blue scarf was writing on the blackboard. She turned around. "Good morning, students. My name is Mrs. Duval." She gave them name tags to fill out. "If you write your names on these, it will be easier for me to learn them. Did Mrs. Wirth tell you she'll be out of town all week?"

"She went to Ohio," Thomas said.

"Yes, she did. While she's gone, I plan for us to work hard, but we'll have fun, too." Mrs. Duval smiled at the class.

Jamaica gave a thumbs-up to Brianna.

"First, we're going to hunt for a hidden object. I hid it in the classroom before you came in." Mrs. Duval gave them two clues: "It's something that lives in Antarctica, and its name starts with the same letter as the object it is hidden in."

All the kids scrambled around the room, except Jamaica. Penguins! she thought. They had read about penguins last week.

She looked at the ledge by the window. She found a plastic penguin in one of the flowerpots.

> To help children identify with Jamaica's desire to impress the substitute teacher, create a character voice for Mrs. Duval that is very soothing and inviting. Use facial expression to help convey Jamaica's variety of emotions.

> Why didn't Jamaica scramble around the room as the other children did? What were the clues that told her where to look?

"Very good, Jamaica. Tomorrow will be your turn to hide an object."

"I'll come early," said Jamaica.

Next they had reading groups.

"Nice job," Mrs. Duval said after Thomas read.

When Jamaica's turn came, she read loud and clear. She knew all the words.

"You read very well," said Mrs. Duval.

Jamaica felt like singing.

In math class they did puzzles. Jamaica had all the right answers. So did Cynthia and Thomas. Mrs. Duval let them choose stickers to put on their packets. Jamaica chose a gray kitten with yellow eyes.

"Cats are my favorite animals," Jamaica told Mrs. Duval.

"I like cats, too," said Mrs. Duval.

How does Jamaica feel about Mrs. Duval?

After lunch Mrs. Duval read a story. Then it was time for spelling.

Oh no, Jamaica thought. She had forgotten about the test.

"Would you like a minute to look over the words?" Mrs. Duval asked.

"Yes," everyone said, except Thomas.

"I know all of the words already," he said.

I wish I did, Jamaica said to herself. She looked at the list and tried to **memorize** every word.

> Do you think Jamaica will do well on the spelling test?

"Time to start," Mrs. Duval said.

The first five words were easy. Then Mrs. Duval said, "Calf."

Jamaica's mind went blank. She chewed on her pencil.

She **stared** out the window. She closed her eyes. I'll never get a perfect paper, she thought. When she opened her eyes, she noticed Brianna's paper. She could see the letters, too. "C-a-l-f," Jamaica wrote on her paper.

> How did Jamaica choose to solve her problem? Was this a good choice?

Then she looked up.

Was Mrs. Duval staring at her? Jamaica looked back down at her paper. What would Mrs. Duval think if she had seen her copy?

"Okay, time to **exchange** papers," Mrs. Duval said, and she put the spelling list on the bulletin board.

Jamaica wrote "100%" on Brianna's paper. Brianna drew a happy face on Jamaica's and put "A++++" across the top.

When Jamaica got her test back, she crossed out the happy face. It's not a perfect paper even if it looks like one, she thought.

"Please pass your spelling papers to the front," Mrs. Duval said.

Jamaica put hers in her desk.

> Why do you think Jamaica didn't pass her paper to the front?

Next came art, Jamaica's favorite class, but she couldn't think of anything to draw.

"Jamaica, could you come here for a minute?" Mrs. Duval said.

Jamaica got up and walked slowly to Mrs. Duval's desk.

"Your spelling test isn't with the others, Jamaica. Did you hand it in?"

Jamaica shook her head. "I can tell you my score."

"I'd like to see it," Mrs. Duval said.

Jamaica showed her the paper. "It should say 'minus one.' I missed 'calf.' "

" 'C-a-l-f ' is right," Mrs. Duval said.

"But I didn't know how to spell it," said Jamaica. "I copied." Jamaica started to explain why she wanted to get a perfect paper, but it was too hard. "I'm sorry, Mrs. Duval," she said.

> Do you think it was hard for Jamaica to tell Mrs. Duval what she had done?

"I know," said Mrs. Duval. "It wasn't easy for you to tell me you copied." Mrs. Duval's voice was low, almost a whisper. "You know, Jamaica, you don't have to be perfect to be special in my class. All my students are special. I'm glad you're one of them."

"You are?" said Jamaica.

Mrs. Duval nodded.

"So am I," said Jamaica. "I hope you can be our substitute teacher again."

Jamaica sat back down at her desk and began to draw, but she didn't have time to finish her picture. She took it home and colored in the gray kitten and Mrs. Duval with her hundred braids. Then she wrote, "For Mrs. Duval from Jamaica." Tomorrow she would give her picture to Mrs. Duval. Tomorrow, first thing, she would hide an object in the classroom.

Jamaica couldn't wait.

Talking About the Story

- Ask children to tell what they think Jamaica learned during her day with the substitute teacher.
- Invite children to share experiences they have had with substitute teachers or other adults, such as coaches or club leaders, whom they have wanted to please.

Vocabulary in Action

memorize

In the story Jamaica tried to memorize the spelling words. When you memorize something, you make sure that you know it without having to look back at it. Let's say *memorize* together.

- Ask which you might want to memorize, the words to a song or what you ate for dinner last night. Explain.
- Draw a triangle, circle, and square on the board. Ask children to memorize the shapes. Cover them and call on a child to name them and tell what order they are in.

stare

Jamaica stared out the window while she tried to remember how to spell *calf*. When you stare, you look straight at something for a long time. Let's say *stare* together.

- Ask which would be fun to stare at, a pretty painting or a blank wall. Why?
- Ask children to choose an object, such as their shoes, and to stare at that object while you count to 10.

exchange

The class exchanged tests to check them. When you exchange something, you give something to someone and they give you something, too. Let's say *exchange* together.

- Ask which you would want to exchange, an old pair of shoes for a new pair of shoes or a new pair of shoes for a handful of mud. Explain your answer.
- Have children exchange a book or a pencil.

Words About the Story

relief

Jamaica felt much better after she told Mrs. Duval about what she did on the test. Another way to say this is that Jamaica felt relief. Relief is what you feel when you get rid of something that has been bothering you or when you finish something that was difficult. Let's say *relief* together.

- Ask children when they might feel relief, when they get lost in a store or when they are found after getting lost in a store. Why?
- Have children give a sigh of relief, wipe their brows, and say, "Whew!"

regret

Jamaica felt bad about copying on the spelling test. She regretted what she had done. When you regret something, you wish you had not done it. Let's say *regret* together.

- Ask children if they would regret missing a chance to meet a famous singer or getting something they wanted, like the lead in the school play. Explain why.
- Ask a child to show how they would look if they regretted having lost their favorite book.

anxious

Jamaica was worried that Mrs. Duval might not like her. Another way to say that is that Jamaica felt anxious. If you feel anxious about something, you are worried about what might happen. Let's say *anxious* together.

- Ask if children might feel anxious walking in the woods at night or walking through the kitchen in their home. Why?
- Ask children to act out what they would say to someone who was feeling anxious about flying in an airplane to help that person feel calm.

And to Think That We Thought That We'd Never Be Friends

In this story in rhyme, people stop arguing and turn into a huge parade of friends!

Vocabulary

Words From the Story

These words appear in blue in the story. You might wish to go over their meanings briefly before reading the story.

commotion
A commotion is a lot of noise and people moving around.

fret
When you fret about something, you look and act as if you are worried about it.

soothe
When you soothe someone who is angry or upset, you calm them down.

protest
When you protest something, you make a show of saying that you are against it.

Words About the Story

These words will be introduced after the story is read, using context from the story.

conflict   **harmony**

Getting Ready for the Read-Aloud

Show children the picture on pages 144 and 145 of the big parade. Read the title aloud, and explain that this story tells about people who are having arguments or fights. But when they join a special parade, they make up and become friends.

Tell children that the story mentions the Pied Piper. According to an old fantasy tale, the Pied Piper led rats away from the town of Hamelin. The Pied Piper played his pipe, and all the rats followed him and the sound of his pipe.

You can explain the following words and concepts as you come to them in the story: *din*, a loud noise; *squabbled*, had a fight; *cacophony*, a terrible sound.

And to Think That We Thought

By Mary Ann Hoberman
Illustrated by Kevin Hawkes

One day we were playing outside in our yard
When my brother got mad and he pushed me so hard
That I pushed him right back—with all of my might—
And quick as a wink we were having a fight!

That We'd Never Be Friends

We thwacked and we whacked and we
walloped away,
And we still might be fighting to this very day,
Pinching and punching, my brother and I,
If only our sister had not happened by.

Bringing the Story to Life

Read the parts about fighting with
intensity and the parts about making
up in a gentler tone. As the parade
gains momentum and becomes
larger, increase the excitement in
your voice.

She was sipping some soda pop out of a cup,
And she said she would share it if we would make up;
And since we were thirsty and tired and sore,
We each took a drink and we ended our war.

It's funny how quickly an argument ends…
And to think that we thought that we'd never be friends!

How did the fight begin?
How did the fight end?

That night after supper we turned on TV,
But we couldn't agree on what show we should see;
I wanted one and my sister another,
And both of us hated the choice of our brother.

And we probably all would be arguing yet
If our dad hadn't come in and turned off the set.
So we put on pajamas, curled up on his bed,
And he read us a wonderful story instead!

It's funny how quickly an argument ends…
And to think that we thought that we'd never be friends!

A day or two later, it wasn't much more,
A great big new family moved in right next door;
How many were in it we couldn't quite tell,
But they each played an instrument—not very well!

One played a tuba and one a bassoon.
They practiced all morning and all afternoon.
They practiced all evening and all through the night,
And they kept us from sleeping, and that wasn't right.

So we got out of bed with a hippety-hop,
And we marched off together to beg them to stop.
But when we arrived there, they asked us to play,
And they did it so nicely that what could we say?

I took a whistle, my sister a flute,
And my brother a trumpet that gave a loud toot.
My dad took a bugle, my mother a drum,
And we all forgot totally why we had come!

It's funny how quickly an argument ends...
And to think that we thought that we'd never be friends!

> How did this argument end?

Then all of a sudden we heard a loud blare
As a siren came wailing from out of thin air!
A police car pulled over, out jumped the police,
And they told us that we were disturbing the peace;

And they said if we didn't stop playing that minute,
They'd take us to jail and put all of us in it!
My brother got red and my sister grew pale,
And everyone trembled at going to jail.

But my mother explained that the noise we had made
Was because we were practicing for a parade;
And she said that the siren had sounded so grand
That she hoped they would ride at the head of our band!

It's funny how quickly an argument ends...
Now all of the police had turned into our friends!

We marched down the street, and each person we passed
Loudly complained at our earsplitting blast.
They begged us to deaden our deafening din
Until we invited them all to join in!

We offered them boxes and kettles and spoons,
And once they were playing, they all changed their tunes!
They all were so pleased by the music we made
That they became part of our splendid parade.

> What does "they all changed their tunes" mean?

More and more people stepped right into place,
More and more people kept up with our pace,
Strutting and striding and stamping their feet,
Marching in time to the drums' steady beat.

Friends who had squabbled and even stopped talking
Settled their differences once they were walking,
Smiled at each other and marched hand in hand,
Keeping the beat of our wonderful band.

And then we could hardly believe what we saw—
Dog and cat enemies marched paw in paw!
And when our procession arrived at the zoo,
Lions and tigers joined in with us, too!

It's funny how quickly unfriendliness ends...
And to think that we thought they could never be friends!

Our music was magic, a magnet to all,
As to a Pied Piper, they came at its call;
And as we kept marching and tooting and drumming,
The people kept coming and coming and coming!

Hundreds and thousands came running to find us!
Thousands and millions fell in right behind us!
What a cacophony! What a **commotion**!
Then all of a sudden we got to the ocean.

We came to the place where the whole country ends...
With hundreds and thousands and millions of friends!

Oh, what could we do now? We started to **fret**.
We couldn't keep marching without getting wet.
Then just as we all began turning around,
We heard a most odd and unusual sound.

It wasn't a moan and it wasn't a cry.
It wasn't a groan and it wasn't a sigh.
It was more like a hum humming high up the scale,
A whisper, a whistle, a whimper, a wail.

A wail? No, a *whale*! Yes, a hundred or more!
And all of them swimming straight into the shore,
Singing their whale songs and grinning with glee,
So we jumped on their backs and sailed straight out to sea!

Sharks swam around us while baring their teeth!
Stingrays kept rising from far underneath.
But somehow the songs and the music we played
Convinced them to join in our ocean parade.

For music is magic, it **soothes** and it mends.
And to think that we thought that we'd never be friends!

What happened when the parade reached the ocean?

We crossed the wide ocean and washed up on land,
Where people kept hearing the sound of our band.
And even the ones who first came to **protest**
Soon were parading along with the rest.

And it's hard to believe, but I swear it is true,
By the time we were finished and finally through
And we'd all gotten back to the place we first played,
The whole world was marching in one big parade!

And before we disbanded and each went our way,
We voted to march every year on that day—
To march side by side with the friends we had made
And the friends we'd made up with in one big parade!

And from that day to this that is just what we do,
With the police siren blaring and horns tooting, too,
With our pots and our pans and our trumpets and drums,
And everyone, everyone, *everyone* comes!

And this is our cheer every year when it ends:

Forever and ever, we'll always be friends!

Talking About the Story

- Ask children to describe the different fights and arguments and how people made up. Have children tell how the parade grew bigger and bigger as more people and animals joined in.

- Invite children to talk about arguments they have had with friends or siblings. Ask if they made up and became friends again. Was it easy to make up? Would they rather fight or be friends?

Vocabulary in Action

commotion

In the story there was a commotion when thousands of people and animals joined the parade. A commotion is a lot of noise and people moving around. Let's say *commotion* together.

- Ask when there would be a commotion, when a lot of people are talking to each other at a party or when two people are reading quietly in a library. Why?
- Ask the class to give you a three-second demonstration of what a commotion would sound like.

soothe

The music from the parade soothes the sharks and the stingrays. When you soothe someone who is angry or upset, you calm them down. Let's say *soothe* together.

- Ask which would soothe a girl who just fell off her bike, her friends zooming right by her or helping her up and making sure she's okay. Tell why.
- Have a child pretend to soothe a puppy that's scared.

Words About the Story

conflict

In the story people have arguments about different things. Another way to say that is to say people have conflicts. When two people or two sides have a conflict, they can't agree about something and have a big argument. Let's say *conflict* together.

- Ask who is having a conflict, two people who fight about what to cook for dinner or two people who cook dinner together. Why?
- Ask two children to act out having a conflict about what game they should play.

fret

The people and animals in the parade began to fret when they reached the ocean. When you fret about something, you look and act as if you are worried about it. Let's say *fret* together.

- Ask children who is fretting, a girl who has to eat a brownie or a girl who has to eat dirt. Explain your choice.
- Invite children to describe some things that make them fret.

protest

Some people came to protest the noise the band was making. When you protest something, you make a show of saying that you are against it. Let's say *protest* together.

- Ask children if you protest eating lima beans, do you want to eat them or not. Explain your answer.
- Ask children to talk about some things that they would want to protest.

harmony

The people who had been arguing came to-gether to make beautiful music. They made mu-sic in harmony. Harmony is created when different sounds come together to create beautiful music. Let's say *harmony* together.

- Ask which makes harmony, a group of people who are playing violins well or a group of people tapping their foot on the ground. Explain why this is.
- Play a tape of a cappella harmony, or call on a group of children to sing together in harmony.

Bibliography

Ahrens, Robin Isabel. (1988). *My Building*. Illustrated by Ilja Bereznickas. New York: Winslow Press.

Baer, Edith. (1980). *Words Are Like Faces*. New York: Random House.

Billings, Henry & Melissa Stone. (1994). "World's First Talking Cartoon" from *Headlines of the Century: 1920–1929*. Austin, TX: Steck-Vaughn.

Clements, Andrew. (1988). *Big Al*. Illustrated by Yoshi. New York: Simon & Schuster.

Cooper, Patrick. (1998). *Never Trust a Squirrel!* New York: Dutton.

Cote, Nancy. (1998). *Flip-Flops*. New York: Albert Whitman.

Foreman, Michael. (1996). *Seal Surfer*. San Diego: Harcourt.

Hamilton, Martha, & Weiss, Mitch. (1999). *How & Why Stories: World Tales Kids Can Read and Tell*. Little Rock, AR: August House.

Havill, Juanita. (1999). *Jamaica and the Substitute Teacher*. Illustrated by Anne Sibley O'Brien. Boston: Houghton Mifflin.

Hoberman, Mary Ann. (1999). *And to Think That We Thought That We'd Never Be Friends*. Illustrated by Kevin Hawkes. New York: Random House.

Kleven, Elisa. (1992). *The Lion and the Little Red Bird*. New York: Dutton.

Lobel, Arnold. (1980). *Fables*. New York: HarperCollins.

Nichol, Barbara. (2001). *One Small Garden*. Pittsburgh: Tundra Books.

Prelutsky, Jack. (2002). *The Frogs Wore Red Suspenders*. New York: HarperCollins.

Prelutsky, Jack. (1978). *The Queen of Eene*. New York: HarperCollins.

Prelutsky, Jack. (1980). *Rainy, Rainy Saturday*. New York: HarperCollins.

Robson, Chelle. (2003). *The Tortoise and the Baboon*. Austin, TX: Steck-Vaughn.

Root, Phyllis. (2000). *Kiss the Cow!* Illustrated by Will Hillenbrand. Cambridge, MA: Candlewick Press.

Rosa-Casanova, Sylvia. (1997). *Mama Provi and the Pot of Rice*. Illustrated by Robert Roth. New York: Atheneum Books.

Rupp, Rochelle. (2003). *Coyote and the Stars*. Austin, TX: Steck-Vaughn.

Sierra, Judy. (2002). *Silly & Sillier: Read-Aloud Rhymes From Around the World*. New York: Knopf.

Tibbitts, Tina. (1988). "Mr. Bizbee and Miss Doolittle" from *Marvin Composes a Tea*. Columbus, OH: Highlights.

Turner, Teresa. (2003). *Strong Enough*. Austin, TX: Steck-Vaughn.

Viorst, Judith. (1997). *Alexander and the Terrible, Horrible, No Good, Very Bad Day*. Illustrated by Ray Cruz. New York: Atheneum Books.

Additional Favorite Read-Alouds

Anderson, Laurie Halse. (1996). *Turkey Pox*. Illustrated by Dorothy Donohue. Morton Grove, IL: Albert Whitman.

Duncan, Alice Faye. (1999). *Miss Viola and Uncle Ed Lee*. Illustrated by Catherine Stock. New York: Atheneum Books.

Ernst, Lisa Campbell. (1992). *Walter's Tail*. New York: Simon & Schuster.

French, Vivian. (1994). *Red Hen and Sly Fox*. Illustrated by Sally Hobson. New York: Atheneum Books.

Hayles, Karen. (1993). *Whale Is Stuck*. Illustrated by Charles Fuge. New York: Atheneum Books.

Hest, Amy. (1996). *Jamaica Louise James*. Illustrated by Sheila White Samton. Cambridge, MA: Candlewick Press.

Kimmel, Eric A. (1994). *Anansi and the Talking Melon*. Illustrated by Janet Stevens. New York: Holiday House.

Pfeffer, Wendy. (1995). *Marta's Magnets*. Parsippany, NJ: Silver Press.

Prelutsky, Jack. (1996). *A Pizza the Size of the Sun*. New York: HarperCollins.

Sweeney, Joan. (1998). *Bijou, Bonbon & Beau*. Illustrated by Leslie Wu. San Francisco: Chronicle Books.